Arabic Speaking Communities in American Cities

Edited by
Barbara C. Aswad

D0162251

CENTER FOR MIGRATION STUDIES OF NEW YORK, INC.
ASSOCIATION OF ARAB-AMERICAN UNIVERSITY GRADUATES, INC.

The Center for Migration Studies is an educational, non-profit institute founded in New York in 1964 to encourage and facilitate the study of sociological, demographic, historical, legislative and pastoral aspects of human migration movements and ethnic group relations everywhere. The opinions expressed in this work are those of the authors.

ARABIC-SPEAKING COMMUNITIES IN AMERICAN CITIES

A joint publication of the Center for Migration Studies of New York, Inc. and the Association of Arab-American University Graduates, Inc.

First Edition

Cover design by Kamal Boullata

Copyright © 1974 by
The Center for Migration Studies of New York, Inc.
All rights reserved. No part of this book may be reproduced without written permission from the publisher.

Center for Migration Studies
209 Flagg Place
Staten Island, New York 10304

ISBN 0-913256-12-9
Library of Congress Catalog Card Number: 73-88936
Printed in the United States of America

The Contributors

MAY AHDAB-YEHIA is a doctoral student in Sociology at Wayne State University, Detroit, Michigan.

BARBARA C. ASWAD is Associate Professor of Anthropology at Wayne State University, Detroit, Michigan.

PHILIP M. KAYAL is Assistant Professor and Chairman of the Department of Sociology, Seton Hall University, South Orange, New Jersey.

LEILA B. SABA holds a MA in Sociology from Wayne State University.

MARY C. SENGSTOCK is Associate Professor of Sociology at Wayne State University, Detroit, Michigan.

CHARLES L. SWAN is Associate Professor of Sociology at Wayne State University, Detroit, Michigan.

LOUISE E. SWEET is Professor and Chairman of the Department of Anthropology at the University of Manitoba, Winnipeg, Canada.

ALEYA ROUCHDY is Assistant Professor in the Department of Near Eastern Languages and Literature, Wayne State University, Detroit, Michigan.

LAUREL D. WIGLE is a doctoral candidate in Anthropology at Wayne State University, Detroit, Michigan.

Preface

The intention of this book is to bring together several previously unpublished social science studies about people from the Arabic-speaking Middle East who live in American cities. It is not meant to be an encyclopedia of all the activities, clubs, churches mosques and associations of the nearly two million Arab immigrants and their descendents, but is meant to add to the sparse literature that is available on this relatively small minority. It may in that way add to our research so that we may someday compose such a complete study.

The editor is pleased to have the support of the Association of Arab-American University Graduates in the publication of their second book of studies on the Arab American Community (the first was edited by E. Hagopian and A. Paden, 1969). And she is especially pleased that the Center for Migration Studies is co-publishing the book. She would like to particularly thank Dr. Philip Kayal who is a contributor to this book and a member of the Editorial Review Board of the Center, for his help in the final editing of these essays.

Table of Contents

*Arabic Speaking Communities
in American Cities*

Introduction and Overview

The interest and revival of ethnic groups in themselves and in other ethnic groups has become pronounced in the late 1960s and 1970s. The Arabic speaking community is no exception. The once popular theories and slogans of the melting pot and assimilation grew into those of blending by religious affiliation, pluralism and ethnic revival within a context of class structure and dominance. The fact became obvious that many members of ethnic groups in America had not lost their pride in their cultural values and customs, and perhaps in response to the success of the new expression of cultural identity by the dominated Black societies, and in addition to a need for identity in the troubled period of social fragmentation during the war years of the 1960s, we find ethnic revitalization.[1]

In the case of the Middle Eastern communities, however, we cannot look only to the conditions existing in the complexities of urban American life. Part of the stimulus for ethnic reemergence is from the outside, caused by the conflicts in the Middle East itself, and the American communities' growing alienation from U.S. national policies which have heavily supported Israel in and since its creation in 1948.[2] Another factor we may mention is the continued and increased connections between the communities here and those in the Middle East. In part this is due to the continuing in-

1

troduction into the communities of refugees and immigrants from the Mid-East. The establishment of inexpensive air charter flights has also provided more frequent communication than had ever been thought possible. These trips are welcomed by most Middle Eastern countries as boosts for their economies. Thus communication networks which had never really been severed, are strengthened, old relationships reestablished and new ones created.

Because Middle Eastern Arabic speaking peoples share a common historical and cultural heritage generally, and because there is a common cultural revival and interest in their heritage, they may be chosen as a basis for a book. However, there are numerous subgroups within this broad category of peoples and the immigrants do not reflect all the social groupings in the Middle East. In fact most come from one region of the Middle East and are of a religious minority status in the broad area of the Mid-East. One of the smallest religious categories in the Americas is that of Sunni Muslims, the religious affiliation of the vast majority in the Arab world. Approximately ninety percent of the immigrants and their descendents are Christians from the Lebanese region. Christians number about six percent in the Arab world, but significantly, within the state of Lebanon, they are not a minority since they form approximately half of that population and hold positions of strong political and economic power. The role of religious categories as social groups operating within a class structure is far more important in a country like Lebanon than for example Egypt where the vast majority belong to one religious sect. Nevertheless we shall pay some attention to this factor as it is operative in this country.

In the area of socio-economic class, we find that the majority of the immigrants, Muslim and Christian alike, came neither from the elite nor the sharecropping classes, but from towns or villages in the rural areas where most owned some property in the form of kin units and were dependent upon their crops for subsistence as well as for cash. Some were small merchants, or combined these functions. Many Lebanese villages are considered prosperous and the people more literate than numerous other villagers in the Mid-East. In addition, due to the association of Lebanon with foreign trade, many towns and villages are influenced by contacts of their members with foreign countries in Africa, Latin America and the

North Americas. In general they initially became peddlers, farmers and small merchants in the areas to which they migrated.[3] Later some became larger merchants, white collar workers and professionals. Money was sent back to relatives, marriages were arranged and communications continued.

The fact that most migrants are of minority status, a few of refugee status such as the Palestinian refugees, and in recent times some are members of the educated "brain drain" phenonema, relates to a combination of the following factors: the history and geographical location of these groups, to their relations with past empires and with the dominant industrialized West, as well as to the rise of nationalism in the Middle East and to Western immigration policies which at various times have favored categories of relatives, skilled persons and refugees. The priority given to relatives by these policies resulted in a process known as "chain migration" so that certain kin groups and villages or towns have a high percentage of immigrants clustered in certain regions. In general, most early immigrants (those in the late 19th and early 20th Centuries) planned to stay in the West only long enough to earn money and return to their villages or towns. A number of factors prevented this and most settled down, brought their relatives here and raised families. A different type of migration is seen however, in the case of the Yemanis where primarily men have come to work, save money and return to Yeman (see Aswad paper). In all cases, significant amounts of money have been sent back to relatives. In most of our studies, the importance of family and extended kinship relations is clear. One has only to be in the Middle East a short time to be aware of the importance of these units socially, economically and psychologically. Although there are varieties of relationships, they have been found essential in the process of migration and adaptation, particularly initial adaptation, and operate within the contexts of other social units such as the community or religious association.

Let us consider briefly the position of minorities under the Turkish Ottoman and Western Empires (mainly British and French), and then discuss the specific position of Lebanon. The official religious affiliation of the land-based Ottoman regime, which ruled the region for four hundred years until the end of World War I, was

Sunni Islam. In areas of direct governmental control such as cities, sea coasts and plains, religious minorities usually served in merchant positions. In areas of indirect control, such as mountainous regions like Lebanon or peripherial areas, both Christian and Muslim minorities held varied positions including political, landowning and peasant statuses. Religious minorities were also found along certain ecological or ethnic boundaries.

In the mid-19th century, European colonial powers began to gain economic power in the Mid-East and undermine Ottoman control. By the end of World War I, the Western states carved up the Arab world by drawing national boundaries, and then took official political control of the regions through Mandate and Protectorate power. In their policies of control, they favored and established ties with several social categories. One was the rich landowning elites, another the merchant and minority groups. Thus, although the Middle East is part of the basically agrarian regions which became dominated by the expanding industrial powers, not all groups became involved in this process in the same fashion. Some cemented links with the West, some were extremely exploited by it, particularly groups such as the poor peasants of Egypt who provided cheap labor to pick cotton for British textile mills. Later, numerous sectors resisted the domination. Most Middle Eastern countries did not receive their politcal independence until after numerous struggles and the end of World War II. The rise of nationalism as a reaction to Western control, placed pressures on social groups that had sided with the West. This was also combined later in some countries with pressure on merchant groups by socialistic governments.

It was during the period of British colonial rule in Palestine, and increasingly after the atrocities of World War II in Europe, that we find the migration of Europeans of Jewish faith and the eventual Zionist occupation and wars which resulted in the creation primarily by Western powers of a Jewish state in 1948, and the consequent displacement and impoverishment of most Palestinians. Today the number of Palestinians is over two million. Since the 1967 War and further Israeli occupation of Arab lands, we now find new refugees, Palestinian as well as Syrian and Egyptian. The peasantry and lower classes became the most dispossessed, but other Palestinians found themselves often in a position of a resented minority in other countries. The reader is referred to Sharabi (1962, 1966, 1969) for further discussion of these historical periods in the Arab world.

Within this general historical framework, Lebanon has a specific history and social organization. It is characterized by a decentralized organization based to a high extent upon numerous religious sects and a strong emphasis upon kinship and village affiliation. These social categories operate within a class system in which some of the elites have been rural based as well as urban based. (In most areas of the Middle East, dominant elite classes are urban based). In the mid-19th century Lebanon was a prominent silk producer and came under French economic influence. During the four hundred years of Ottoman rule and before, its mountainous terrain provided a region for religious minorities. When the Western colonial powers entered the area, the various religious groups became highly politicized. The French extended educational, economic and political ties to the Catholic Maronites, one of the largest religious sects in Lebanon. The Russians favored the Greek Orthodox and the British, favoring the Jews and Christians of Palestine, favored the Druze in Lebanon. In Lebanon some religious groups are more numerous and powerful than others, but each is economically stratified within itself. That is there are Maronite merchants, bureaucrates and peasants, there are Druze landlords and peasants.

Elements of structural pluralism are built into the Lebanese society through such factors as the constitution which sets a quota for the numers of members serving from each religious group. High positions are also specified by tradition as to religious affiliation. The President is traditionally a Maronite Catholic, the Prime Minister Sunni Muslim and so forth. Presently the elites of each group, although favoring different political allies and policies, cooperate in the parliament, while parties which cross religious sects among lower and other classes are discouraged or illegal. Thus there is a consensus among the top classes. It should be added however that cross national and cross religious parties have been increasing in strength recently. Religious groups are highly endogamous, that is they marry within their unit To a great extent these religious boundaries correspond with preference for marriage within village or kin units. Civil marriages are seldom practiced in

Lebanon, and intermarriage is usually difficult with conversion required.

Numerous studies and discussions have been made of this system.[4] Some have termed it a mosaic, some a plural society, others emphasize the class aspects. One distinction that seems important to the editor here in comparing a system such as Lebanon and the elements of ethnic revival in America is the distinction between pluralistic and cultural elements.[5] For example in terms of cultural traits, the Maronite and Druze villager are very similar, and certainly share a more similar life-style than either do with members of their elite urban co-religionists. Many of the elements of ethnic revival in the U.S. emphasize shared Middle Eastern cultural traits.

In contrast to decentralized Lebanon, we find a country such as Egypt. Organized around intensive irrigation cultivation along the Nile River, its population is dense and historically it has been associated with a highly stratified socio-economic class system until the Nasser regime in the 1950s. The exploitative relationship it suffered under the British resulted in intensification of production and overpopulation, and a depressed standard of living for the vast majority of the Egyptian population, the peasantry. Although there are numerous reforms and planning, Egypt still suffers from the problems intensified during that period.[6] Very few Egyptians have migrated to the West, although there is currently an inflow of members of the primary Christian minority, the Copts.

In other areas of the Middle East, we find such sparsely populated areas as the Arabian Peninsula which have, in contrast to Egypt, rich oil fields. These countries are becoming increasingly powerful, while until forty or so years ago they emphasized herding, shipping and limited agriculture. At the tip of the Peninsula is the mountainous regions and seacoasts of the Yemans, where rainfall is more plentiful and agriculture and shipping predominate. The ecological variety therefore is great between regions in the Middle East, and within regions we find great social differences between classes, between some urban and rural regions and between the variety of towns, cities and villages themselves.

Thus when we look at the dynamics of migration and adapation to a new society, it is obvious that we must consider the conditions and social position of the people in their country of origin as well as the conditions into which they entered. There are also obvious and significant differences according to the time period in which the immigrants arrived and differences between the various generations. The varieties are extensive as we will see in the following essays. The social separations of groups in the home country continue in the new country and influence much of the day to day social activity and attitudes. For example Muslim groups generally identify more with Arab causes and less with the West than say the Catholic Lebanese Maronites. Yet during times of mutual crises or in the social context of groups with different cultural and linguistic characteristics, a sense of ethnicity built on shared cultural traits occurs. One such example of this latter situation is found in the institution of Ethnic Festivals in the city of Detroit. Middle Eastern political situations find the groups reflecting the attitudes and countries of their origin, sometimes bringing unity, sometimes representing differences.

The communities are now part of the class and ethnic system of America, but in different positions. Most entered near the bottom as most immigrants from rural regions do, and many worked and were allowed into positions of upward mobility, others are in the dominated lower classes. A fairly unusual case would be the example of the Ramallah community whose members had a significant degree of education before entering the U.S.

The editor does not wish to overemphasize religious associations. However the factors of class origins and occupations, kinship and national affiliations are discussed in most of the articles. Also, for the reader not familiar with the religious categories represented here, a brief explanation of the history of the Muslim and Christian sects is justified.

The Christian sects are numerous and sometimes confusing to the Westerner. A diagram is provided in the appendix which shows the major schisms and their approximate dates.[7] We may summarize here the two major splits which resulted in the numerous Christian sects. The first schism occurred when the various national sects left the Orthodox Byzantine Church because of doctrinal divergences or political disputes. Most of these occurred between 431 A.D. and 680 A.D. This resulted in the formation of the Nestorian, Old Syrian (Jacobite), Armenian, Coptic and Abyssinian Churches.

Together with the Orthodox Church, they are now called the "Independent Eastern Churches". The second split occurred after the major division of the Roman Catholic Latin West from the Greek Orthodox East in 1054 A.D. Each of the Independent Eastern Churches had a splinter group which reunited with the Roman Catholic Church and they were collectively called the "Uniates". The group that split from the Nestorian Church was called the Chaldean Church, those that split from the Eastern (Greek) Orthodox were called Greek Catholics (often called Melkites), from the Old Syrians came the Syrian Catholics, from the Armenian Church came the Armenian Catholics, from the Coptic Church, the Coptic Catholics, etc. The Maronites, although becoming close to Rome in 1182 A.D., did not effect union until the eighteenth century. They did not split as a church and they claim an uninterrupted communion with the Roman Church.[8] We should mention that there are very few Protestants in the Middle East, although some were converted in mission schools.

In Islam, there are two main divisions, the Sunni and the Shia. The great split took place in the first century of Islam and the origin of the split involved the political control of the Arab Empire. The major rivalry was between Ali, the fourth Caliph and cousin and son-in-law of the Prophet Muhammad, whose capital was at Kufa in Iraq, and Muawiya of the Umayya family of Mecca who had moved his capital to Syria. The supporters of Ali became the Shia and after his fall the sect became involved in a social struggle against the aristocracy. The Sunni are divided into four schools of law, but these are not important in their organization today in most areas. The Shia are divided into four subdivisions that are separated by geography and on the issue of the last in the line of Imams. In the Arab world, the Sunnis outnumber the Shia, however in Lebanon the relative proportion of Shia is high. One article in our book discusses a Druze community from Lebanon. This sect was founded in the eleventh century and which most scholars agree is greatly influenced by the Ismaeliya Shia sect.

There are other communities and subgroups in America which are not represented in our collection. Some have been previously discussed in other publications. The type of migration involved in the "brain drain" phenonema is well discussed by Suleiman (1969), and it is important to mention that these educated immigrants as well as the students in universities have had an important part in the political and cultural revival of the American communities. They differ somewhat from the communities in that many are not of rural backgrounds, and thus often do not have as extensive village, town or kin ties here. Also many tend to be from upper classes rather than lower classes.

Overview of Essays

When scholars choose to conduct a study, they tend to pick one subcultural group, or to conduct a cross sub-cultural analysis. The papers in this collection represent primarily the first category, that of looking at one localized sub-cultural group. Some are distinguished primarily by religious identification such as the Maronites of Detroit, some by the origin of their village or city in the home country, such as the Ramallah community, some by their special location and socio-economic status in this country, such as the South End auto workers of Dearborn. Most communities share a combination of these factors, a common geographical origin, a common religious faith, a common general location, and a general occupation or class level.

Turning to the communities in America and their similarities and differences, the distinction made in the article by Swan and Saba regarding types of ethnic communities in the U.S. is a valuable one, and we can use it to classify the studies. In category one, we find the "Ethnic Enclave" which is described as a geographically localized community built on primary relationships, and maintaining a high degree of economic and some political control within the community. An example of this type of community is the Amish in the U.S. We do not have an example of such an enclave in our studies. In category two, they list "Ethnic Neighborhoods or Ethnic Primary Communities." These resemble the first type in their geographical localization and close social relationships, but the main economic and political controls are outside the community. The Muslim community of auto workers in the South End of Dearborn would fit into this category (see Aswad and Wigle articles.). The third category is termed "Ethnic Secondary Communities" and is characteristic of most of the other groups discussed here. In this class there is no compact geographical clustering although there is often a larger regional clustering, and the community is a voluntary association organized around a church, or other type of association. The Maronites (article by Yehia) and the Ramallah community (Swan & Saba), fit this category. The fourth category is that of an "Ethnic Public" in which the population is scattered but retains "an interest" in ethnic affairs and expresses their interest primarily in the public through the mass media and pressure groups. It seems that this category is somewhat weak among the Arabic speaking population due to the strength of category three, but such a trend is emerging through organizations which cross-cut type three groups. One of these is the Association of Arab-American Graduates, another is the newly created Arab-American Immigrants.

The reader will notice that many of the studies deal with communities in the Detroit region. This is due to several factors, one is that the Detroit community is one of the largest Arabic speaking centers in the U.S. with over 70,000 members, and it is also due to the fact that an increasing number of studies are available on this community. Because of this, a map has been provided of the metropolitan region so that the reader may be able to identify the locations discussed in the papers. A brief mention can be made here regarding the general characteristics of Detroit's ethnic movement as it relates to specific communities.

It is a fact of Detroit ethnic and class history that various groups have moved from the central city along street corridors which fan into the suburbs. The move accompanied both the expansion of businesses into these areas and the increased accessability of transportation. It also was a negative reaction to the increasing Black population in the center city, the members of which were barred from residing in the suburbs. The ethnic groups formed what we have referred to as secondary ethnic communities and ethnic publics in the suburbs. In most cases, the movement was accompanied by a rise in occupational, economic and educational status.

The Arabic speaking population, followed this pattern, and its movement resulted in a dispersion primarily according to religious divisions. But we must remember that these divisions are also similtaneously divisions which generally correspond to regional and

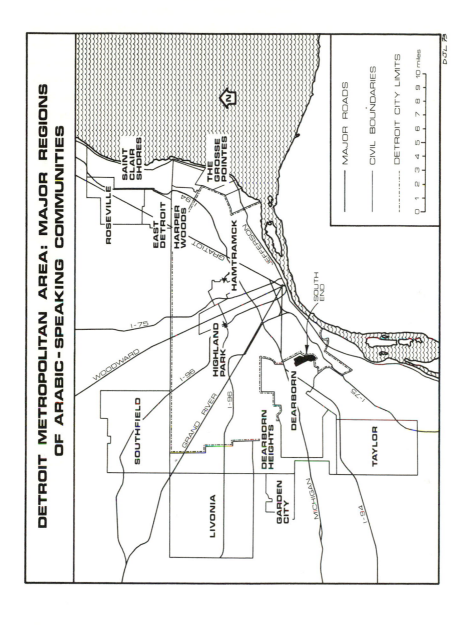

DETROIT METROPOLITAN AREA: MAJOR REGIONS
OF ARABIC-SPEAKING COMMUNITIES

MAJOR ROADS

CIVIL BOUNDARIES

DETROIT CITY LIMITS

0 1 2 3 4 5 6 7 8 9 10 miles

SAINT CLAIR SHORES

THE GROSSE POINTES

ROSEVILLE

EAST DETROIT

HARPER WOODS

HAMTRAMCK

GRATIOT

JEFFERSON

SOUTH END

I-75

HIGHLAND PARK

WOODWARD

I-96

SOUTHFIELD

DEARBORN

I-94

GRAND RIVER

I-96

DEARBORN HEIGHTS

MICHIGAN

LIVONIA

GARDEN CITY

TAYLOR

DJL 75

kinship groupings in the home country. Thus, most Maronites moved out Jefferson Ave. and now live in East Detroit and the adjacent suburbs of Roseville, Harper Woods and the Grosse Pointes. The Chaldeans originally settled in central Detroit and Highland Park and migrated to north Detroit and the northern suburb of Southfield. Recent Chaldean immigrants live in Detroit and Highland Park. Most Muslims (Southern Lebanese, Palestinians, etc.) had settled in central Detroit and Highland Park around the first Ford Assembly plant, and moved to Southeast Dearborn near the Ford Rouge Plant when it was constructed in 1924. This community has remained a region which continuously receives Muslim immigrants, and is the only Middle Eastern community in the Detroit region whose members are primarily of the unskilled laboring class. In recent years some of its Yemani population has been moving to Hamtramck where they work in Chrysler plants. Some upwardly mobile persons have moved from the South End of Dearborn to its higher income western section and other western suburbs. The Ramallah community, immigrating somewhat later than the other groups and having educational, occupational and language skills which provided mobility, are fairly scattered but to some extent they live in the general region of Livonia and Garden City. [9]

Let us now consider each study briefly.

In Sengstock's paper we find the interesting case of a small minority in the Arab world, the Catholic Chaldeans of Northern Iraq and Baghdad, who have successfully established themselves in an occupational niche in Detroit. Although there are other aspects of their organization not discussed here but which can be found elsewhere (Sengstock 1967), this paper has focused on one of the most fundamental factors, the economic, which has contributed to their maintenance of identity and their adaptation to U.S. culture. Their occupation was at one time almost totally restricted to the retail grocery business in central Detroit. As members became successful, Sengstock discusses their movement and mobility. The editor might add that the ·community of Telkeif straddles a boundary between two Muslim ethnic groups, the Kurds and the Arabs in northern Iraq. Also, historically some of the members of this community served as middlemen in the sable fur trade between

Russia (via the Kurds) and the British. Later some members also served in the colonial British bureaucracy in Baghdad. Thus, in some ways, elements of their pre-migration social situation can be seen as a preadaptation to serving in a merchant niche in the U.S. ghetto area. The recent influx of new members in large numbers is providing some stress in the community since the nature of the economic niche is changing. The maintenance of small retail stores in the ghetto has become a dangerous occupation, and many of the older members are more affluent now. There has been some effect of separating the community (Bannon 1972).

Sweet's study well describes the method by which a Middle Eastern village community reconstitutes itself in an industrial society. Having studied the Druze village in Lebanon and the community in Canada, she is particularly qualified to make comments on this experience. Her writing also reflects many of the emotions that are felt in this communion. The recent cause for migration from the village has been due to the pressures of repeated Israeli bombings and destruction of much of the village in 1972. In general, the experience reflects the principle of chain migration, whereby members of one society follow in chain like fashion to live with their kinsmen or villagemates.

In her study she concludes that the corporate industrialism of Canada and its class structure inhibits mobility and assimilation of those without the proper credentials and "Invites no one to give up his class, family and clan life for the industrial alternative: vagrancy and welfare."

Aswad's study of the lower-middle income working class Muslim community in the South End of Dearborn analyzes the situation of a primary ethnic community that finds itself faced with an attempt to destroy it through "urban renewal" policies which would convert the region to industrial use. The members of this community are primarily from Southern Lebanon, Palestine and Yeman. The entire geographical community of five thousand persons is located under the Ford Rouge stacks and has other ethnic groups in it, however, its core and flavor are Middle Eastern. There are coffee houses, a mosque and religious hall, plus numerous Arabic restaurants and grocery shops which serve the community. The author reviews the closeness of primary social and economic ties in the community and their positive sentiments toward it. She also discusses the relationship of this area to the rest of Dearborn and to Ford, and the history of the struggle with the City to prevent its destruction. Most recently the community brought a class action legal suit against the city and a Federal judge found that the City was using illegal means to destroy the community. The situation of struggle by a weaker force against a City the nature of Dearborn created divisions within the community as well as provided a new organization, and in many ways the struggle is found to be analygous to those of imperialized or colonized communities.

Swan and Saba's paper concerns a community that has migrated from the small city of Ramallah, Palestine. One of the distinctive features of this community is the high level of pre-adaptation to Western customs through the Quaker school and the positions of some in the government of the British Mandate in Palestine. Their members belong to the Greek Orthodox, the Greek Catholic and Protestant Churches and thus there is no one ethnic church. However, they were a Christian minority and in some ways are similar to the Chaldeans, although the closeness of their town to the cosmopolitan Jerusalem, their advanced educational backgrounds and knowledge of English gave them credentials for a different type of mobility in U.S. society. Most received their educations in Palestine or a combination in that country and the U.S. Today 24% are professionals, 13% managers and 41% are in white collar jobs. (Saba 1971:114) The community is a secondary community and has a very high rate of endogamy (75%). This endogamous rate includes people from Ramallah who live in other parts of the U.S. as well as in the Detroit region itself. The authors find that most left to find better employment, but also the pressures of the Palestine War in 1947, the rise of nationalism and the occupation of Ramallah by Israel in 1967 gave further impetus to continued migration. The community retains a strong interest in their country and town and the authors discuss aspects of their identification.

Kayal addresses himself to the history of Syrian and Lebanese Christians as a minority and their relationships to the established Christian Churches in the West. Their position as a minority has made it difficult for them to totally identify with Arab culture and causes. However to totally integrate with the Western churches meant for the Catholics to Latinize, and this they feared would mean the demise of their religious tradition and a threat to their community. Thus he notes a compromise in which they lived a dual life style, in public they assimilated and religiously were latinized, in private they maintained elements of their own identification.

His data is taken from his study of the Melkite community in Brooklyn and his article principally concerns the Catholic Communities of Lebanon and Syria, and Maronites and Melkites. He does not deal with the Eastern (Greek) Orthodox communities except to say that they faced similar problems. It might be added that in the Middle East, the Orthodox were not tied as closely to Western policies as the Catholic communities. Kayal states that while publically assimilating to the Western religious churches, distinctiveness if often found by marrying other Christians of Arab background.

Yehia's study of the Maronite community in Detroit tells us of the first settling of this community in the heart of Detroit and its migration to the eastern suburbs, as some members went from occupations of small retailers and industrial workers to that of realtors and insurance brokers. Many of the second generation became professionals.

This community is the largest community from the Middle East in Detroit, numbering approximately 20,000. Yehia found that her respondents appear to be highly assimilated into American culture. Most have American names, the majority speak English at home, and most identify themselves as American Lebanese. It is a secondary community whose members belong to clubs related to the Maronite Church and to their villages of origin as well as to larger Lebanese societies. She finds a high rate of endogamy within the religion (81%) and found that none of her respondents had married with other Middle Eastern Catholic groups such as the Melkites or Chaldeans, but rather married with other nationality Catholics, such as Italians. Perhaps the difference in her marriage figures and Kayal's high rate of out-marriage by the Syrian Melkites is due to the larger size and concentration of the Maronite group both in the U.S. and Lebanon, versus the smaller size and concentration of the Melkites in the U.S. and Syria.

Wigle's study also concerns the South End Muslim community of Dearborn. She analyzes the four variables of kinship, religion, community and nationality. She argues for the importance of the extended family, a notion contrary to some previous ideas that industrialization is associated with the break-up of the large family. She states that it has been modified but is essential. She also notes the position of the Zaim, or influencial politician and its adaption to local politics. Islam she finds is strongly associated with the other variables, and is associated with the political events in the Middle East. The identification of persons in this area as Arabs is stronger than in most of the previous communities, however, there are also distinctive nationality affiliations which form sub-groups in the community. Finally she finds, as did Elkholy in an earlier study (1966), that among the third generation there is a new emphasis upon Arab culture which is stronger than the somewhat assimilationist trend of the second generation.

Lastly, Rouchdy, as a linguist and native speaker of Arabic, has studied the effect that Arabic has on English and vice versa among bilingual Arab American children in the South End of Dearborn. She found that bilingualism does effect the subject's performance in Arabic and English and that we cannot judge performance unless we consider both domains of the bilingual. She also concludes that since Arabic is the socially dominant language in that community, it ought to be part of the school curriculum there.

The bibliography on Arab-Americans has been primarily composed by Dr. Kayal, and is intended to provide the reader who is interested in pursuing this area of study further with a basic list for reading and research.

Areas for further research

It is important to mention that a book of this nature does not portray all the sparkle, warmth and spirit of the communities, a spirit that is represented for example in the Arab Ethnic Festivals in Detroit. The beautiful colors of Arab dresses and dances, the food, and the pride that is evident in all the various groups as they work separately and jointly in that successful event of four days, relates to the rise of ethnic feeling among the groups, and is seemingly a trend toward the emergence of a stronger single identity among the groups. In this vein, I am sure that many members of the communities discussed here may feel while reading these essays that, "this isn't how we live, these are mainly numbers." Both types of reporting are necessary and we may hope that in the future, additional articles will also be written about life in the communities to supplement these.

It is also felt by the author that there is room for comparative studies, that is comparative studies of sub-groups such as these, as well as comparative studies with other ethnic groups according to criteria of class or other background materials such as urban rural differences, etc. so that we may get additional understanding of the processes and strategies involved in adaptation to American life and international life. Analysis of this type should also focus on the effect of migration on the community which the migrant has left. Thus while the majority of our studies here show the facet of adaptation here, the process is one of interaction, and future studies might attempt to include the total environment of the immigrant communities.

Barbara C. Aswad
Detroit 1973

NOTES

[1]For discussion of these theories see among others, Gordan (1964). Feinstein (1971), Gans (1962), Laumann (1973), Glazer & Moynihan (1963).

[2]In some cases there have been reports of harassment of Arab-Americans by U.S. authorities since "Operation Boulder" was initiated by the U.S. Government in 1972. ("U.S. Harassment of Arabs Continues", AAUG Newsletter, 1973).

[3]See Hitti (1924) for an interesting and thorough discussion of the early migrants.

[4]See among others, Gulick (1965, 1971), Suleiman (1965), Hudson (1968), Barakat (1973).

[5]See Gordan (1965, ch. 6), Singham (1971), Depres (1970) Wax (1973) for discussions of cultural and structural pluralisms.

[6]See Abdel-Malek (1968).

[7]For a general discussion of the various theological beliefs of Christian and Muslim sects the reader is referred to Hitti (1951), Hourani (1946) and Baer (1964 ch. 3). For their ecological distribution in Lebanon see Gulick (1965).

[8]Hitti (1951: Ch. 32).

[9]Needless to say, these settlement patterns found in Detroit are not necessarily found in other American cities.

BIBLIOGRAPHY

Abdel-Malek, Anouar
    1968   Egypt: Military Society. New York: Vintage.

Bannon, J.
    1973   Adaptive Interaction Patterns: The Chaldean Case. Detroit:
            Wayne State University, Dept. of Anthropology (Unpublished
            Paper).

Baer, Gabriel
    1964   Religious and Ethnic Groups. Chapt. 9 in, Population and So-
            ciety in the Arab East. New York: Praeger.

Barakat, Halim
    1973   Social and Political Integration in Lebanon: A Case of Social
            Mosaic. The Middle East Journal. 27:3, 301-318.

Barth, Frederick (ed.)
    1969   Ethnic Groups and Boundaries. Boston: Little Brown.

Despres, Leo
    1970   Differential Adaptations and Micro-cultural Evolution in Gu-
            yana, in Afro-American Anthropology. N. Whitten and J.
            Szwed (eds.), New York: The Free Press.

Feinstein, Otto (ed.)
    1971   Ethnic Groups in the City. Lexington Mass: Heath Lexington
            Books.

Gans, Herbert
    1962   The Urban Villagers. New York: The Free Press.

Glazer, Nathan and Daniel P. Moynihan
    1963   Beyond the Melting Pot. Cambridge: M. I. T. Press.

Gordon Milton
    1964   Assimilation in American Life. New York: Oxford University
            Press.

Gulick, John
    1965   The religious structure of Lebanese culture. Internationales
            Jahrbuch fur Religionssoziologie 1:151-187.

    1971   The Arab Levant, in The Central Middle East, L. Sweet (ed.),
            New Haven: Human Relation Area Files.

Hagopian, E. and A. Paden
  1969   Arab-Americans. Wilmette: Medina University Press Interna-
          tional.

Hitti, Philip K.
  1924   The Syrians in America. New York: Doran Co.

  1951   History of Syria. New York: Macmillan.

Hourani, A.
  1946   Minorities in the Arab World. London: Oxford University
          Press.

Hudson, Michael
  1968   The Precarious Republic: Political Modernization in Lebanon.
          New York: Random House.

Jackson, J. A.
  1969   Migration. Cambridge: Cambridge University Press.

Laumann, Edward O.
  1973   Bonds of Cultural Pluralism: The Form and Substance of
          Urban Social Networks. New York: Wiley.

Mitchell, J. Clyde
  1969   Social Networks in Urban Settings. Manchester: Manchester
          University Press.

Saba, Leila
  1971   The Social Assimilation of the Ramallah Community Residing
          in Detroit. Unpublished M.A. Thesis. Wayne State University.
          Detroit.

Sharabi, Hisham
  1962   Governments and Politics of the Middle East in the 20th
          Century. Princeton: D. Van Nostrand.

  1966   Nationalism and Revolution in the Arab World. Princeton: D.
          Van Nostrand.

  1969   Palestine and Israel: The Lethal Delimma. New York: Pe-
          gaesus.

Singham, A. W.
  1971   The Political socialization of Minority groups, in Majority and
          Minority, N. Yetman and C. Steele (eds.), Boston: Allyn &
          Bacon.

Suleiman, Fuad
   1973   A Topical Bibliography of the Arab-Israeli Conflict 1917-1971.
           Columbus: Forum Associates.

Suleiman, Michael W.
   1967   Political Parties in Lebanon. Ithaca: Cornell University Press.

   1969   The New Arab-American Community, in Arab-Americans, E.
           Hagopian and A. Paden (eds.), Wilmette: Medina University
           Press International.

"U. S. Harassment of Arabs Continues"
   1973   Association of Arab-American Graduates Newsletter, 6:4,p.7.
           Box 85, N. Dartmouth, Mass.

Wax, Murray
   1973   Cultural Pluralism, Political Power and Ethnic Studies, in
           Learning and Culture. American Ethnological Society: Seattle:
           University of Washington Press.

Weaver, Thomas and P. White (eds.)
   1972   The Anthropology of Urban Environments. Monograph 11 of
           the Society for Applied Anthropology. Seattle: University of
           Washington Press.

Yetman, Norman R. and C. Hoy Steele (eds.)
   1971   Majority and Minority: The Dynamics of Racial and Ethnic
           Relations. Boston: Allyn & Bacon.

Young, Michael and Peter Willmott
   1957   Family and Kinship in East London. Baltimore: Routledge and
           Kegan Paul.

Iraqi Christians in Detroit: An Analysis of an Ethnic Occupation

MARY C. SENGSTOCK

A major sphere of activity for the analysis and understanding of human behavior in complex, industrialized society is the economic sphere: the manner in which men make their living. As Everett C. Hughes points out, "Race, sex, marital status, and other characteristics formerly determined civil estate quite directly; now it is work that counts . . . ., and the other characteristics take their importance by virtue of their influence on one's place in the labor force." (Hughes, 1959, p. 443.) In the world today, the occupation by which one makes his living determines to a great extent the manner in which he lives. This is true for several reasons. For one thing, one's occupation, in modern society, largely determines one's economic status, which in turn places a limit upon the style of life a man can enjoy; hence occupation, in this respect at least, is central to the entire manner of living he can pursue. In addition, gainful employment occupies the greater part of the waking hours of men, and increasingly of women also, in American society. Hence an analysis of their occupational activities is an important part of the analysis of any group.

With regard to an immigrant group, the occupational pattern followed by the members of that group can have substantial and far-reaching effects upon the members of the group and the group itself. Since so much of men's lives are spent in the occupational

21

sphere, since the rest of men's lives are largely dependent upon the remuneration obtained in his gainful occupation, a study of the economic pattern of an immigrant group can tell us much about the group itself. Many immigrants experience their first and most shocking contact with the culture of their new lands when they are forced to seek jobs with strangers in a strange country. Fortunate indeed is the immigrant who can find a job among his own—who discovers that those who preceeded him in emigration from his native country have established an economic network in the land of his destination. Such a network will allow him to earn a living in the new setting among people who share ties with his ancestral home-land, speak his language, understand his culture and aspirations, and can ease his adaptation to the strange new setting.

An outstanding example of an immigrant group which has es-tablished a substantial ethnic economic structure is a group of Iraqi immigrants in the Detroit area. Nearly all members of the com-munity come from the same town, Telkaif, which is located near the City of Mosul in Northern Iraq, south of the Turkish border (Sengstock, 1967, 1970.). This section of Northern Iraq differs from the Iraqi nation in general, in that residents of the area are largely Christian rather than Moslem. As Christians in a predominantly Moslem region of the world, villagers in this area have endured the often unpleasant status of a minority. Many authorities have pointed out that relations between Christians and the dominant Moslems in the area have at times been strained, to say the least (Badger, 1852, p. 163; Longrigg and Stoakes, 1958, pp. 23-29; Adeney, 1965, p. 496).

The religious history of the area is further complicated by the existence of several different varieties of Christianity in the region. Most Christian residents of the area historically were followers of Nestorius, a bishop and prominent teacher in the Eastern Christian Church who was censured by Rome in the fifth century for preaching doctrines at variance with accepted Catholic doctrine (Attwater, 1947, p. 98). In the period since that time, many Nes-torians have reunited with the Roman Catholic Church, forming an Eastern rite called the "Chaldean rite" (Adeney, 1965, pp. 497-498; Attwater, 1947, Vol. I, p. 199; King, 1948, II, pp. 251-290; Addis and Arnold, 1964, p. 135). In the past two centuries, Protestant missionaries have also visited the area (Badger, 1852, pp. 178-181). According to community informants, residents of Telkaif were among the Nestorians brought into the Chaldean rite around 1830.

The language of the Chaldean rite is a modern version of ancient Aramaic, the language Christ spoke. Residents of Telkaif speak a dialect of the Chaldean church language which they proudly call "Jesus language." Most immigrants today are conversant in Arabic, the dominant language of Iraq. Many also speak Kurdish, an Indo-European language. This is due to the fact that Telkaif is located on the border between the Kurdish and Arabic speaking ethnic groups in Northern Iraq. Services in the Chaldean Church in Detroit are variously offered in the Chaldean (Aramaic) language, Arabic, and English for American-born Chaldeans. Members of the community are proud of their union with Rome, and identify closely with their village and religion. Most members of the community prefer to be called "Chaldeans" or Telkeffees (in Aramaic, "Telkeppees"), rather than "Arabs" or "Iraqis," although pro-Arab sentiment in the community is growing.

The earliest immigrants from Talkaif arrived in Detroit around 1910-1912. By 1923 there were ten members of Detroit's Iraqi community: Joe John Assar, George Essa, Tobia (Thomas) Hakim, Thomas Kory, Namo Kaca, Namen Losia, George and Louis Najor, David Orow, and Tom Peter. By the time the study of the community was conducted in 1962-63, the population had grown in size to 344 nuclear families, with approsimately 2,000 persons (Sengstock, 1967, p. 113). The community is still growing at a considerable rate. In 1966, the community listed 450 nuclear families, with about 3,800 persons (Directory, 1966, p. 14). By 1972, it had grown to 1,187 nuclear families and 5,900 persons (Directory, 1972, p. 4). There may be an additional one to two thousand persons not registered with the Church. Part of this growth is, of course, natural increase. But much of it is due to continued immigration. Such immigration has increased in recent years with the new, less restrictive American immigration laws. Prior to 1965, Iraqi immigration to the United States was limited to 100 persons per year. At that time, new legislation was adopted by Congress which was much more liberal in its immigration allowances (C.Q. Almanac, 1965, p. 459.).

A few Iraqis from other villages were also living in Detroit. But the source of growth of the community has been primarily Telkaif, or descendants of emigrants from Telkaif living in Baghdad, Mosul, or other parts of the world. The community has retained a high degree of contact with the original village and with Telkeffes living elsewhere (chiefly Baghdad and Mexico). Marriages and visiting between these various Telkeffe communities are frequent. In a community census conducted by myself in 1962, only eight of the 305 families whose village origin was known were from Iraqi villages other than Telkaif. Thus the community of Iraqi immigrants in Detroit is essentially from a very localized part of Iraq.

Contact between Detroit's Chaldean community and other Arab immigrants to the United States has been quite limited. In the early years, Detroit's Chaldeans had some contacts with Syrian and Lebanese immigrants, most of them Christians like themselves. One of the early Chaldeans reportedly purchased a grocery store from a Syrian predecessor. And early Chaldean immigrants frequently attended religious services at Detroit's Lebanese Maronite Church, St. Maron's. Once their own parish, Mother of God, was established in 1947, the ties between Lebanese and Chaldeans in Detroit became less frequent. Ties to Detroit's Muslim Arab community have been less frequent, even almost non-existant at times. But there have been reports of increases in such ties in very recent years.

The earliest Chaldeans in Detroit lived on the near East Side, near Jefferson and East Grand Boulevard, an area also populated at that time by other Arabic Christians from Lebanon. As the communities grew, however, they tended to diverge, with the Lebanese continuing to move eastward into Grosse Pointe and St. Clair Shores, the Chaldeans moving to the West Side of Detroit and Highland Park, and into the Northwest suburbs, chiefly Southfield. The inner city Church which served the community for many years was sold in August, 1972. Groud-breaking for the new Church, located at Ten Mile Road and Berg Road, in Southfield, Michigan, was held on June 25, 1972. The Church was dedicated on May 15, 1973, by the Chaldean rite Patriarch from Baghdad. Chaldean rite services are also held at St. Rita's Roman Catholic Church in Detroit for Chaldeans who live in the central city.

Members of the Detroit community today include not only the

immigrants but their children born and reared in America. Today, a third generation, the American-born children of American-born Chaldeans, are beginning to play a part in the community. The major groups today still consist of the immigrants and the second generation. Throughout analysis of the community, I have refrained from use of the term "American-born." On the assumption that the locus of the early years of family life and education are more important than the actual place of birth, Chaldean immigrants were distinguished from the American-*reared* rather than American-*born*. "American-reared" Chaldeans included Chaldeans born and reared in the United States, as well as Chaldeans born in Iraq but brought to the United States before the age of ten years. It was assumed that children brought to the United States at this early age would remember little of their experiences in Iraq and be exposed primarily to American customs as a result of their American school experiences.

The Chaldean Economic Community

As has been mentioned, one of the early Chaldean immigrants was introduced to the grocery business by a Syrian immigrant from whom he purchased a store. Thus began a community ethnic occupation which has grown and prospered to the present. In the 1962 community census, over half of the nuclear families received the bulk of their support from the retail grocery business or its allied industries. Many of these stores were small—the type commonly referred to as the "Mom and Pop" store—owned and operated by one man assisted by his wife and children. Such stores carry a limited stock, give credit on a small scale basis to their customers, and are open long hours, from early morning to late night.

However, the Chaldean grocery business has been increasingly expanding beyond this level. In several instances, grocery store owners have found it helpful to form partnerships with other store owners. This allows them to open a larger store, have more and varied stock, obtain supplies at greater discount, and draw a larger clientele. Also important is the fact that each owner is then allowed more free time, as his partner can be depended upon to operate the store for a part of each day.

In addition, Chaldean businessmen have expanded into the

wholesale food industry. Chaldeans owned 120 grocery stores of various sizes in 1962. It is obvious that this constitutes a sizeable population for the purchase of wholesale supplies. Hence some Chaldeans have founded wholesale grocery businesses. Two wholesale milk and ice cream distributorships are owned and operated by Chaldeans. Others owned linen supply firms, or distributorships for snack foods, notions, or other commodities. In addition, a large number of Chaldeans, especially new immigrants, were able to obtain employment with non-Chaldean wholesale food suppliers, who hired them on the assumption they could obtain the not-insignificant Chaldean market.

In an ethnic group which has a complex and widespread economic operation, profound effects are produced on all other aspects of the ethnic group life. The family, ethnic organizations, the ethnic Church, the cultural life of the people—all are closely tied to the occupation by which the bulk of the members make their living. The remainder of this article will be devoted to discussing some of the effects which the Chaldean ethnic occupation have had upon the Chaldean community.

The Ethnic Occupation and the Family

The Chaldeans of Detroit have their origins in the traditional, non-industrial community of Telkaif. In such a community, the extended family plays a most important role (Al-Nouri, 1964, Chap. 1.). Retention of Chaldean social patterns depends, to a great extent, upon their ability to maintain close ties among family members—including grandparents, aunts and uncles, and cousins, as well as the parent-minor child tie stressed in the industrialized United States.

The existence of a strong economic tie in the Chaldean community has served as an aid to the retention of strong family ties. Grocery store owners find their job becomes easier when they join forces with relatives. Hence many Chaldeans make their living in close cooperation with relatives: father and son, two brothers or brothers-in-law, uncle and nephew, or cousins often form partnerships in economic ventures. Nearly forty percent of Chaldeans who had adult relatives in Detroit were engaged in business ventures with them. They are able to maintain closer family ties in this setting. This encourages a close tie between family members, who see each other and work together everyday. Clearly, the opportunity to work closely with relatives in an ethnic occupation aids in maintaining the close extended family ties of the traditional Chaldean life style.

In addition, these business establishments provide an employment opportunity for relatives and friends in Iraq who wish to immigrate, for they are assured of a job on their arrival. Brothers, cousins, and friends, can obtain employment in the retail stores or wholesale grocery firms of Chaldeans. This function of the grocery business in facilitating Chaldean immigration is well recognized in the community. Often respondents stated they intended to establish a store precisely for the purpose of bringing family members from Iraq. One Chaldean engineer left his profession to open a store, because it increased his ability to help relatives and friends join him here. The advantage to immigrants of any independently-owned business, whether it be a grocery store, cleaning establishment, restaurant, et cetera, is obvious. The man who owns such a store can put his relatives and friends to work helping him, obviating the necessity to hire other personnel. Thus they become an economic asset to him immediately upon their arrival in America. Their lack of English is not even a problem, since he can help them by translating. However, when a man employed in a large corporation brings relatives to join him, he cannot easily obtain employment for them, especially if they do not know English. Hence they can contribute nothing to their own support, and constitute only a financial liability to the relative who brought them. Hence an ethnic occupation aids the immigrant and his family by providing him with a means of contributing to his own support.

An additional indication of the role of the ethnic occupation on Chaldean families can be found in the reasons why Chaldeans chose their occupations. Chaldean respondents who were asked why they had selected a particular job gave a large variety of responses: some chose a position because it offered a large income; others because the job was secure; some because they found their positions interesting or challenging. But a full twenty-five percent mentioned family-oriented reasons for their job selection: their fathers had wanted them to take a particular job; an uncle, brother, or cousin had needed help in his business; and so on. Interestingly, this tendency to consider extended family needs and wishes was more characteristic of American-reared Chaldeans than of immigrants, a fact which should surprise many Chaldean parents who claim that their children brought up in America do not respect the Chaldean family traditions. (Sengstock, 1967, pp. 224, 259).

This is not to imply that the retail grocery business has any sort of "magical quality" among Detroit's Chaldeans. It would be inaccurate to suggest that Chaldeans enter the grocery business because of an interest in the business itself. Some do find the work interesting, of course, but most are drawn to it precisely because of its ethnic and familial ties. The early immigrants had had many occupations in Iraq before emigrating, including many types of entrepreneurial jobs. Upon their arrival here they searched for a suitable occupation, but any of a number of occupations might have sufficed. As was noted earlier, Chaldean entry into the grocery business was almost accidental, occasioned by a Syrian predecessor's sale of a store to one of the early Chaldean immigrants. Had this early arrival chanced upon someone selling a restaurant rather than a grocery store, the Chaldeans might have established a different economic pattern.

Once established, however, the grocery business became largely self-perpetuating, primarily because it became a part of Chaldean family structure. Initially, immigrants became grocers because it was an available occupation, and not too difficult to learn. Before long, however, new immigrants were becoming grocers for an additional reason, the desire to work with relatives. Further, second-generation Chaldeans also were joining the business to help fathers and uncles. Again, the motive was not primarily a desire to enter the grocery business, but rather a desire (or perhaps a feeling of obligation) to work with the family. It is clear that the family and occupation are closely intertwined in the Chaldean community. The existence of an ethnic occupation helps to maintain close family ties. And conversely, family ties help to draw young people into the ethnic occupation.

Community Cohesiveness and the Ethnic Occupation

The effect of an ethnic occupation extends not only to the family but to the community as a whole. Just as families are drawn together by a common economic venture, so the Chaldean community as a whole is drawn together too. Chaldean stores tend to be clustered in specific areas of the innter city of Detroit. Half of them were in census tracts with more than one Chaldean store. This close proximity of store location has a twofold effect upon the community.

One consequence is the generation of considerable intra-community rivalry and competition. When businesses of the same type are located so close together, drawing upon the same clientele, competition for business is inevitable. Consequently, there is considerable, sometimes fierce competition among Chaldean store owners for customers. This tends to perpetuate old family rivalries from Telkaif and generate new ones.

At the same time, however, the proximity of stores helps to increase community consensus by encouraging informal social contact with other Chaldeans. Over half of the Chaldeans in the grocery or related businesses told me they visited other Chaldeans at their stores more than once a week. Some of these were business calls by wholesale suppliers or their employees to solicit and deliver orders; many others were purely social calls. But all help to increase community cohesion by increasing the number of social ties Chaldeans share.

Besides serving as an informal visiting network, it should be obvious that the Chaldean ethnic occupation operates as an informal ethnic welfare association. I have shown how it provides jobs for community members as store employees (though many Chaldeans employ non-Chaldean workers also), and how it provides a source of clients for Chaldeans in the wholesale grocery trade (nearly all Chaldean retailers bought at least a part of their stock from Chaldean suppliers, and this constituted a substantial part of the business of Chaldean wholesalers). Such help is clearly of greatest importance for new immigrants who require an immediate means of support, though it is used also by some second generation Chaldeans. Apparently, a need for the security of an ethnic occupation grows less important as members of the community are established in American culture and society.

The existence of an ethnic occupation thus serves to unite the ethnic community more closely, since it provides an additional setting in which members of the ethnic group can meet and interact. Raymond Breton, in a study of ethnic populations in Montreal, Quebec, noted that ethnic communities which had several formal institutions were more able to retain a high frequency of informal personal contact among their members (Breton, 1964). In Detroit's Chaldean community, the ethnic occupation fulfills the function of such an institution.

Chaldeans who are engaged in grocery or allied occupations are more likely to have married endogamously and be living near other Chaldeans than are their countrymen in other occupations. As Table I shows, 88 percent of Chaldeans in the grocery or allied business were married endogamously, and the same percentage resided in areas which were major concentrations of Chaldean households. The corresponding figures for Chaldeans not in the grocery business were considerably lower: only 70 percent of the non-grocers were married endogamously, and 77 percent were living in Chaldean settlement areas.

Chaldeans who share all three of these traits, like the ethnic populations in Breton's study (1964), were likely to exhibit many other traits of Chaldean social structure and culture as well. In Table II I have listed five aspects of ethnic activity, and indicated the likelihood of participation in each. Members of the community have been divided into three groups, depending upon their occupation, marital type, and household location. Anyone who was related to the ethnic community on all three variables (e.g., was em-

TABLE I
Household Location and Marriage Type
by Occupation

		Occupation		
		Grocery or Allied Industry	Other	
A.	Marriage Type (ϕ = 0.348): Endogamous	87.8%	69.6%	(N = 249)
B.	Household Location (ϕ = 0.152): Chaldean Settlement	88.1	76.6	(N = 266)

ployed in a grocery or related industry, married to a Chaldean, and living in a Chaldean settlement) was rated "high" on the Index of Ethnic Community Participation (E.C.P.). Those who exhibited only two of these characteristics were rated "medium;" anyone with less were rated "low" (Sengstock, 1967, Chap. VIII).

As the Table indicates, there is a direct relationship between these three traits and participation in the other aspects of Chaldean life. Chaldeans with a "high" rating were most likely to speak the Chaldean or Arabic language with their peers. They were more likely to prefer the Chaldean rite and to attend services at the Chaldean Church. They had informal visits with other Chaldeans more often, and more of them belonged to the official Chaldean organization, the Chaldean-Iraqi Association.

Hence the ethnic occupation is playing an important role in the unification of the Chaldean community. It brings Chaldeans together, encourages them to use their language and other shared cultural traits, and in general, helps to integrate members of the Chaldean population into a more closely knit community.

TABLE II
Selected Ethnic Traits by
Index of Ethnic Community Participation

	Ethnic Traits	INDEX* High	Medium	Low	
A.	Use Foreign Language with Peers	77.8%	64.3%	13.3%	(N = 47)
B.	Prefer Chaldean Rite	88.2	60.0	28.6	(N = 46)
C.	Attend Chaldean Church at least once/month	76.5	53.3	13.3	(N = 47)
D.	Visit Chaldeans at least once/week	77.8	53.3	40.0	(N = 48)
E.	Member of Chaldean-Iraqi Assn.	50.9	37.0	13.6	(N = 246)

*Index composed of three (3) variables: Marriage Type, Household Location, Occupational Type.
   High = Exhibits ethnic pattern on all three (3) variables
   Medium = Exhibits ethnic pattern on two (2) variables
   Low = Exhibits ethnic pattern on one (1) or no variables

The Chaldean Economic Community—
An Informal Social Structure in Transition

To this point the description of the Chaldean economic system and its effect upon the community may have given the impression of a highly unified, stable structure of occupational activity. This is true only in part. The Chaldean economic structure includes three major elements: a high frequency of persons in a single occupation; a tendency for the family to work together in an occupation; and a tendency for members of the ethnic occupation to be more closely tied to the community than persons in other occupations.

It would be inaccurate, however, to picture the Chaldean grocery business as a complex, monolithic structure, with well-defined roles, lines of communication and specific positions of leadership. The internal organization of the Chaldean economic pattern is far less structured. With over one hundred grocery stores in a single metropolitan area, the Chaldean community could form a formidable rival to the large chains, should they choose to operate as a unit. Joint purchase of stock and supplies would enable each store owner to obtain what he needs at lower cost. Cooperative advertising would allow all to reach a larger clientele for less expense. Equally important, group advance planning for the location of new retail stores could maximize coverage of the market and prevent intra-community competition for customers.

There have been a few feeble attempts at such joint ventures, all of them largely unsuccessful. For the most part, every Chaldean grocery store operates as an independent unit: selecting the location, purchasing the fixtures and stock, employing help, advertising. The new owner can count on suggestions or perhaps a loan from Chaldean relatives or friends, but essentially he operates as an isolated unit. There is no formal structure to instruct and guide him, or to unify his efforts with those of other Chaldeans. Consequently, members of the community have expended a great deal of money and effort competing with each other for customers, effort which they could have directed as a unit against the major grocery chains: Allied, Kroger, A & P.

There are some indications, however, that this highly informal pattern may be giving way to a more formally structured pattern. There are also hints of a more diversified occupational pattern.

These trends are being brought into the community by two groups: second generation Chaldeans, reared in the United States, and new immigrants, who have come to the United States since the end of World War II.

Born and reared on different sides of the globe, these two groups would seem to be a world apart. But in fact, second generation Chaldeans often find greater community of interests with recently arrived immigrants than they have with their own parents. To attribute this phenomenon to a "generation gap" is an oversimplification and merely avoids the problem. What recent immigrants and American-reared Chaldeans do share is a common cultural background quite different from the first Chaldean immigrants to America. Most young Chaldeans, whether reared in the United States or Iraq, have grown up in a complex, urban, industrialized society. While the early immigrants, for the most part, in the peasant village of Telkaif, recent immigrants are primarily of urban origin. Most have been born, or at least reared in Baghdad. The industrial urban complex of Baghdad shares many characteristics with the industrial urban complex of Detroit. Hence persons reared in each setting, though they may speak different languages and owe allegiance to different political systems, have many experiences in common.

Both have had the benefit of formal education, which was extremely limited in Telkaif. Both have learned, through their experiences in a diversified society, to deal with persons of varied cultural and social backgrounds; in Telkaif, all shared a common heritage, so the early immigrants lacked this experience. Lastly, Telkaif residents depended upon close informal social ties, which made complex formal organization unnecessary; Baghdad and Detroit residents, however, have had much experience with complex, formal organizations, in which the members are only peripherally known to one another. This alternative culture which young Chaldeans, American and Iraq-reared alike, bring into the community has had several consequences.

Diversification of Occupation:

Chaldeans most likely to exhibit the "small retail store" pattern are the earliest immigrants, those who came to the United States before the Second World War. Eighty percent of this group is in the grocery or allied trade. For the more recent immigrants, this figure drops to two-thirds; for American-reared Chaldeans, to forty-five percent. American-Chaldeans and recent immigrants are thus moving out of the grocery occupation. While self-employment was the dominant pattern of the earlier immigrants, recent immigrants and American-reared are more likely to be employed in large bureaucratic corporations. (Sengstock, 1967, pp. 183-186).

Among those still carrying on the ethnic occupation, fewer recent immigrants and American-reared were store owners: slightly over half of these groups, as compared with three-fourths of the older immigrants. With the American-reared, this again signals a trend toward diversification; in this group, one-fourth had moved from retail sales to wholesale food.

The variant approach of the new immigrants and American-reared can be seen even among those who have remained in grocery retailing, for their merchandising methods are quite different from those of the pre-War immigrants. Members of the earlier group are most likely to establish separate independent stores. This is less true of the other two groups. Recent immigrants, in particular, are likely to establish large, supermarket-type stores, than small "Mom-and-Pop" stores. For these ventures they often form partnerships or corporations with other Chaldeans. Older immigrants, if they needed money, most often preferred to use a family source: borrowing from parents, an uncle or brother, Recent immigrants and American-reared prefer to bypass family sources for a formal loan from a bank or loan association. In addition, the few attempts at inter-store cooperation, all of which, as I said, have had limited success, have all been led by, and had their primary appeal among members of the post-War immigrant group. The projects were abandoned when their lack of general appeal was observed.

Such evidence seems to indicate that the younger Chaldeans, recent immigrants in particular, are more oriented toward formalized, bureaucratic organization of their economic lives. They consider such tactics more efficient and "good business" practices. As more and more recent immigrants become engaged in the

Chaldean ethnic occupation, and as the pre-War immigrants retire from active business lives, we might expect to see more bureaucratic practices introduced into the Chaldean economic operation.

The Environment and Social Change

Until the past decade, Chaldeans found Detroit to be a hospitable climate for small-scale retail grocery sales. That climate has changed considerably since about 1965. The main factor involved in this change has been the increased irritation of the predominantly black residents of Detroit's inner city toward businesses of all kinds, especially white-owned businesses in their neighborhoods. In July of 1967, Detroit suffered a civil disturbance of major proportions. The major locus of the trouble was the central part of the city, where the bulk of Detroit's Chaldean stores were located. Many homes and businesses, including many Chaldean stores, were damaged or destroyed. (Sengstock, 1968).

Subsequent to the '67 riot, many Chaldeans who had depended upon the grocery trade for their livelihood became uncertain as to the wisdom of this commitment. Of those whose businesses had been destroyed, some did not rebuild. Often these were men who were close to retirement age and felt they could afford to retire. Some had other businesses in addition to the one destroyed and chose not to rebuild. Some, however, returned to their former stores, often because retail grocery sales was what they felt they knew best.

Among young Chaldeans, not yet committed to an occupation, the Detroit riot has almost certainly brought about some changes in plans. Many young Chaldeans who would formerly have listened with interest as their fathers and uncles told them of good opportunities for opening a store, are now searching for other occupations. Further, many fathers who would formerly have advised their sons to become grocers are now advising them against it. Inner city Detroit is now looked upon as a dangerous, inhospitable place, rather than a possible location for a good business.

This less favorable business environment has probably quickened the pace of economic diversification in the Chaldean community. More young Chaldeans than early immigrants had already been moving into other occupations and into education for the professions. Even greater numbers will likely do so now, which leaves the future of a strong Chaldean ethnic community in doubt.

For the present, however, the retail grocery business remains a central focus for Detroit's Chaldean community. A large proportion of the men in the community still own their own stores. Many other members of the community are employed in the stores owned by other Chaldeans. Even among those who are not retail grocers, many depend upon the retail grocery trade for their living, for they are employed as executives, salesmen or delivery men for wholesale grocery firms; and many of these owe their livelihood to the influence of their Chaldean relatives and friends.

Occupational diversification has been occurring in the community, chiefly in the past decade, as third generation Chaldeans and new immigrants have achieved college educations, and employment as doctors, lawyers, engineers, businessmen. But even among these, many have at one time had a tie to the grocery store—having worked in a store in their youth or upon first arrival in America.

This dominant occupational pattern has in large part contributed to the strength of the community tie today, for it brings many members of the Chaldean group together in the all-important economic sphere. The Chaldean community illustrates the manner in which an ethnic occupation can help to mold a strong ethnic community.

BIBLIOGRAPHY

Addis, William E., and Thomas Arnold
  1964   "Christians of Chaldean Pite." *A Catholic Dictionary*. London: Routledge and Kegan Paul.

Adeney, Walter F.
  1965   *The Greek and Eastern Churches*. Clifton, N.J.: Reference Book Publishers.

Al-Nouri Qais Naiman
  1964   "Conflict and Persistence in the Iraqi-Chaldean Acculturation" (Unpublished Ph.D. dissertation, University of Washington, Seattle).

Attwater, Donald
  1947   *The Christian Churches of the East*, rev. ed., 2 vols. Milwaukee: Bruce Publishing Co.

Badger, George Percey
  1852   *The Nestorians and Their Rituals*. London: Joseph Masters. (Republished; Farnborough, Eng.: Gregg International Publishers, Ltd., 1969).

Breton, Raymond
  1964   "Institutional Completeness of Ethnic Communities and the Personal Relations of Immigrants," *American* Journal of Sociology, LXX, pp. 193-205.

C Q Almanac
  1965   *Congressional Quarterly Almanac*, pp. 459-482.

Directory
  1966, 1972 *Mother of God Telephone Directory*. Detroit: Mother of God Parish.

Hughes, Everett C.
  1959   "The Study of Occupations," *Sociology Today*, R. K. Merton, L. Broom, and L. S. Cottrell, editors. New York: Basic Books, pp. 442-458.

Jones, Maldwyn Allen
  1960   *American Immigration*. Chicago: University of Chicago Press.

King, Archdale A.
  1948   *Rites of Eastern Christendom*, 2 vols. Vatican City: Tipografia Poliglotta Vaticana.

Longrigg, Stephen Hemsley, and Frank Stoakes
  1958   *Iraq*. New York: Frederick A. Praeger.

Sengstock, Mary C.
  1967   "Maintenance of Social Interaction Patterns in an Ethnic Group." (Unpublished Ph.D. dissertation, Washington University, St. Louis.)

Sengstock, Mary C.
  1968   "The Corporation and the Ghetto: An Analysis of the Effects of Corporated Retail Grocery Sales on Ghetto Life," *Journal of Urban Law*, Vol. 45, pp. 673-703.

Sengstock, Mary C.
  1970   "Telkaif, Baghdad, Detroit—Chaldeans Blend Three Cul-
          tures," *Michigan History*, Vol. 54, pp. 293-310.

° ° ° ° °

Reconstituting a Lebanese Village
Society in a Canadian City

Louise E. Sweet

It is now well known in the social sciences that in the course of "spontaneous"[1] rural-urban migration from peasant sectors of a society substantial and integrative social institutions are transplanted and migrants do not necessarily live in deculturated anarchy in urban bidonvilles. Less attention, however, has been given to the extent to which migrants from villages actually reconstitute their specific home communities in the urban settings of their migrations (Doughty 1970: 30-46). When this is, in fact, observed to happen new questions arise that call for explanation. Such explanations challenge what seem to me to be a superficiality of criteria of assimilation and acculturation used by sociologists to amass or interpret statistical data (Abu-Lughod 1967:22-32). Even the approval of the persistence of village institutions in the urban scene as buffers or as aids to adjustment do not answer essential and more profound questions of the nature of cultural systems and processes.

Moreover, observing the migrants from a village in their new setting is only part of the problem. Equally important is the effect of migration in the home community. Again, I am not concerned with the usual and expectable effects of remittance benefits, the possible creation of demographic imbalance, and stress upon the functioning of traditional family structure. I am concerned with the interesting fact that the acquired social system of the emigrant

39

colony is also partially reconstituted, in return, in the home community. This certainly, therefore, affects the so-called 'traditional society.' The interplay is complex and I can only touch upon a few aspects here that do not seem to have been matters of great interest in other studies (cf. Mangin 1970, Potter, Diaz and Foster 1967).

Lastly, an important aspect of the specific case I present here is the temporal depth of continuous communication over seventy years between a particular home community in Lebanon and the generations of its migrants when they were abroad. Other aspects are also important, but this continuity seems to be a primary fact, not only for this specific village in Lebanon, but for the Middle East in general. I would guess this to be a primary feature of community processes in the Middle East, since the diffusion and dispersal of Neolithic cultures began from this area. The migration and return process can easily be regarded as an adaptive mechanism of great antiquity, for Middle Eastern communities, but it should not be confused with the invasion and colonization of the Middle East rationalized by an "ideology" of return.

It is the empirical data from my own field work which has had the greatest impact for me. During 1964-65 I lived about 18 months with a family in the Lebanese Druze village of " 'Ain ad-Dayr."[2] The village is centrally located in the Anti-Lebanon mountain range at an altitude of about 5000 feet. The population was reckoned in 1964 by the people of 'Ain ad-Dayr at about one thousand souls. Of these, by my calculations, approximately a fourth of the men of working age (18-50) were at any one time overseas on "labor migration." Some of these men, especially those in Canada, had taken their wives and children with them, in recent years, but in 1964-65 most had not. I spent the summer of 1966 in Edmonton, Canada, teaching at the University of Alberta and associating as closely as possible with the rather large "colony" of men and their families from 'Ain ad-Dayr. These included two sons of the family I had lived with in Lebanon. Immediately after the intensive eight weeks in Edmonton, I flew to the Middle East on a holiday excursion and revisited 'Ain ad-Dayr briefly. In 1969-70, I returned to teach in Lebanon for a year and, because it was a year of great tension at all the borders of Lebanon—and 'Ain ad-Dayr is close to the Syrian border—I visited the village only twice, but met members of the family and other friends from the village on several occasions in Beirut. Early in 1970, I had the unusual opportunity to fly to Edmonton again, very briefly, and I met, fortuitously, in the air terminal, a number of old friends from 'Ain ad-Dayr. Shortly before I left Lebanon the last time in August 1970, I talked to the oldest son of the family. Like other families in the village, he was sending his parents and three of his five sisters to Canada for greater safety. It was at least the fourth time in the 20th century alone that warfare had created refugees from 'Ain ad-Dayr as well as the more continuous flow of migrants seeking their fortunes. Early in 1972 I learned from friends in Lebanon that the village had been struck by three bombs in an Israeli air raid against presumed guerilla camps near it. Lastly, in October, 1972, I visited the family in Edmonton very briefly, but long enough to feel sharply renewed all those nuances of the manners and customs of a Druze family and village life which the ethnographer's experience alone can imprint.

It is from this background that I want to describe briefly and to try to account for the persistence or continuity of all the events and flavor of home village relations of the 'Ain ad-Dayr people who are emigrants to a western Canadian city. I mean this in the most concrete sense. For in the Canadian city it occurs even though the emigrants from the Lebanese village of 'Ain ad-Dayr fill economic and social positions which scarcely correspond to the socio-economic system which still holds in 'Ain ad-Dayr, in spite of considerable change in Lebanon in the twenty years following upon the end of the 2nd World War (1945).

However, in their interactions with each other in Edmonton, all the status etiquette, program of entertainment, visiting rituals, and even the spatial arrangement of individuals in relation to each other in public places and private homes recreates in the finest detail the same kinds of events that occur in home gatherings, work settings, meeting situations, or community gatherings in the home village. The structure of 'Ain ad-Dayr is thus reconstituted in Edmonton. For beyond this level of interaction of persons, the guidelines, the constraints, and the stimuli are the *de facto* social organization of 'Ain ad-Dayr, and the roles inter-relationships, in familial, kinship, peasant or gentry, and host-guest contexts.

I think it is not enough to say that this is not surprising because nearly everyone over 15 years of age in the Canadian city was in fact born and spent his or her childhood in the home village of 'Ain ad-Dayr, and most have returned to visit several times, if not to stay. That is, I think it is surprising and interesting for other reasons which deserve discussion.

Three generations of emigration between 'Ain ad-Dayr and Canada had in 1966 been increasing over the previous decade in this particular western Canadian city and reflected the economic expansion in Canada. The *frequency* of movement between home village and overseas city had also been increasing, with the expansion of the international air transportation system. Members of the community themselves called attention to the greater speed and reliability of communications by mail, cablegram, and even telephone, even though the village, on its high saddle back ridge, had no access by a motor vehicle road until 1963. These, I think, are important and recent environmental attributes that have made specific recreation of the home community possible. Given the air ticket and passport, one can get from the village to the Canadian city in about 24 hours, without stopovers.

The people involved are not unaware of this persistence of their home community in a new context. Rather, they are very aware of it, *both* in Canada and home in Lebanon. In Lebanon, they prepare to emigrate to Canada and emphasize learning English and wearing western clothes and salutations; in Canada, they plan their returns. In the Canadian city the people of 'Ain ad-Dayr form a community which they themselves divide between the "businessmen" and the "workingmen." This, as we shall see, ignores the gentry-peasant stratification of the home village. And in 'Ain ad-Dayr people of the village will say that men come home to the village for final retirement after many years abroad making fortunes, if possible (and several have), because once home in 'Ain ad-Dayr they can enjoy the respect due families of achieved status by success or ascribed status by birth. But in the massive urban societies of the foreign countries of migration they are "nothing" and may meet hostility and discrimination if they are identified as "Arabs." The people of 'Ain ad-Dayr, wherever they are, move easily and peacefully in terms of at least two status systems of community dimensions: that of the contemporary Canadian 'colony.' and that of the persistent one of traditional origin. [3]

Thus the same people, of the same origin, identity, etc. have two coexistent social systems: the Canadian and the 'Ain ad-Dayr-Druze. Both are two class, but they are not identical. One is an adaptive mechanism for the whole to survive both in Lebanon, Canada, and elsewhere in the world. Still more deeply operative in both are the extended family lineages, clans, and factions of 'Ain ad-Dayr in the international network of migration from the village.

Let me sketch these two status systems briefly. In the traditional status system of 'Ain ad-Dayr, the community is composed of a group of families of *mashayx* or aristocratic gentry status who formerly dominated the community primarily by virtue of their control of most of the best land attached to the village. However, two of these families were also closely associated with keeping the *khuwa* or religious meeting place of the pious men and women of the village and with providing the religious leadership of the community. One of the local *za'im* (political leader) families of the district was also formerly resident in the village but had moved to a neighboring village, a decade or so before the early 1960's, and where it still held tenure of all the arable land. To these aristocratic political and sacerdotal gentry families is given the deference and respect traditionally owed their class by the majority of the peasant or *fellahiin* families of 'Ain ad-Dayr. They enjoy precedence in all matters of etiquette: service at luncheons, seating in social gatherings, and salutations. Even though most of these families no longer occupy the power positions of wealth and control of access in land, and some are now very poor, they still enjoy considerable *authority* in the community and are sought to mediate disputes and bring abour reconciliations. Even though a number of peasant men and women are recognized as also among the pious men and women of 'Ain ad-Dayr, this religious sanctity *alone* is not sufficient to equate them with the traditional local *mashayx* families, and *very* few marriages have been made across this line. Those few that have been made suggest, rather, that this traditional allegiance function has been activated in each case, reaffirming the ties between a large peasant clan and a gentry family.

Within the peasant families of 'Ain ad-Dayr there are now a number of very wealthy men, far more wealthy than most of the gentry families, as well as more so than most of the rest of the peasant families of 'Ain ad-Dayr. It is among these families that alliance marriages are beginning to recur in a pattern suggesting a trend toward development of economic class differentiations. Nevertheless, this is part of the *"overseas"* status system and it has *not* displaced the local *traditional* status system: peasants do not yet seek to fill the most important *traditional* political roles of local leadership whether of the Druze community itself or of the national Lebanese parliament. On the whole the peasants support, rather, the traditional leaders. This is not to exclude the possible decline in potency of these traditional roles and the emergence of wholly new ones in the present stressful times.

In the *Canadian* status system involving 'Ain ad-Dayr people, however, we find a different designation of status, the "Businessmen" and their families, and the "Workingmen." (See Table 1) Among the "businessmen"—some 24, according to my records of 1966—five are of gentry families, but they rank with the 'smaller,' not the bigger businessmen, who are all of the peasant class. Among these latter the most influential are a prosperous insurance salesman, and four men who combine partnerships in the management of four neighborhood supermarkets and who have aided a number of the other men who manage such stores. Three men of the gentry families of 'Ain ad-Dayr manage such small supermarkets (two are partners). Two others are in business which is of dubious respectability in Canada, but not as improper in Lebanon (they are not highly regarded by the community at home or abroad and one young woman in 'Ain ad-Dayr eloped with a

TABLE 1
Socio-economic Status of Men from a Lebanese
Druze Village in a Canadian City

In Canada	In' Ain ad-Dayr		Total
	Gentry	Peasant	
Business	5	19	24
Workingmen	1	27	28
Totals	6	46	52

Note: I cannot regard this small sample, for one summer (1966), as conclusive or significant; economic conditions and 'men' in Canada from the village fluctuate too rapidly. By 1972, for example, two of the gentry Businessmen had returned to Beirut, Lebanon, and the occupations and locations of many of the Workingmen had changed about.

Muslim rather than marry one of them to the dismay and shame of her family and the community, but also to the excitement among the women. This rarely occurs in the Druze community.) In the Canadian city two cousins of a gentry family owned their own delivery trucks and pursued what seems to be one of the oldest Levantine occupations in the Americas, itinerant peddling of urban goods in the rural areas.

Among the 28 "workingmen" of the Canadian colony there was one taxi driver of gentry family origin, working for a cab company. The others were of peasant families and were engaged as machine operators or unskilled laborers in bakeries, department stores, municipal works, hospital maintenance—usually in groups of 2's or 3's. One member of such a group is regularly an "old employee" who has sponsored the younger or newcomer into a job in his company. Needless to say there is considerable mobility among the younger "workingmen" as they seek out more congenial or better paying jobs and hope to get into a store management position. From observation at social gatherings and from conversations it became clear that the favor of the leading businessmen of the 'Ain ad-Dayr community was sought by several of the ambitious newcomers. None of the Canadian (nor of other countries) migrants from 'Ain ad-Dayr had yet entered either a profession or professional training in 1966. By 1972, however, one young man had been admitted to the electrical engineering program at the University of Alberta.

Now, so far as the Canadian urban center is concerned, none of the people of 'Ain ad-Dayr is conspicuous for either social or economic status. With the exception of two men (the leading supermarket manager and the manager of an insurance agency) they do not even rank very significantly in the local Arab-Canadian community in general, and can point to those who *are* the leading figures—the Egyptian *imam* of the local Sunni mosque, the Christian president of the Arab-Canadian Friendship Association, and so on. Thus the people of 'Ain ad-Dayr formed "a community" in this western Canadian context which was based on economic differentiation, and which otherwise resembled that of their village of origin in only the most abstract sense of *two classes*. Within *this* system, men of peasant origin are the highest in economic rank; the few gentry occupied only middling positions.

But on occasions that brought villagers together in the Canadian city—'Ain ad-Dayr was recreated. I was able to be present on a number of such occasions and needless to say the experience was one of "the surprise of recognition."

These occasions were of various kinds and I list them in a rough order of most "public" in the general Canadian context, to least:

1. Meeting a young man coming from 'Ain ad-Dayr at the airport.

2. The annual Arab-Canadian Friendship Association Picnic.

3. Stores managed by 'Ain ad-Dayr families.

4. The 'Ain ad-Dayr community gathering, organized primarily to see the slides I had brought from the village.

5. Visits to the homes of Canada of 'Ain ad-Dayr families.

More extended comments on three of these occasions may emphasize the theme of continuity and reconstitution which I pursue here. It can be prefaced by the general observation that the people of 'Ain ad-Dayr keep close track of each other in the Canadian city, just as they do in the village. In the city visiting, telephoning, working together, sharing letters, using the taxi services of their own men in the business, sharing tools, utensils, goods, money, and help go on continuously within the traditional rules of obligation; they do so in 'Ain ad-Dayr Arabic. Everyone seems involved in carrying out tasks to help someone else in the network—get a job, go to the hospital, buy groceries, find a second hand refrigerator, take charge of an "uncle's" store for a few hours, etc. The rate and intensity of such interactions were surprising, once I was able to repeat and extend visits to homes, stores and to listen to the continuous flow of news and the telephone calls.

1. *The meeting at the airport:* some thirty or forty people—men, women, and children—in a dozen cars converged on the airport one Sunday in July and gathered quietly at the passenger exit point in the terminal to meet "Adib." At first some sat quietly in small groups; but as two young men walked from group to group to announce that the plane had arrived, the 'Ain ad-Dayr people moved to an open space near the door through which 'Adib would come. It

was, in fact, a traditional function of announcing that the two young men were performing. The area was fairly crowded by the general public; one or two air terminal security police stood among the group, but were ignored by them. Those who had come were all members of the "clan" to which 'Adib belonged and included the husbands of a few wives who had married into other clans. Men of allied lineages were also there. The men were not saying a great deal among themselves; the women were wondering whether 'Adib's new wife would be with him.

'Adib, whom I had known well in 'Ain ad-Dayr as a close cousin of the family I lived with, was in his early thirties. He was moderately literate in Arabic, with few words of English, of volatile temper (as befitted his status as a defender of the community), and possessed no known skills beyond mountain subsistence farming. He came on a landed immigrant status to join, ostensibly, the un-skilled labor force, sponsored by local kinsmen[4] in fully docu-mented fashion.

Immediately upon coming through the door into the terminal he moved into the circle of 'Ain ad-Dayr welcomers. The Druze etiquette of reception is fairly surprising to a British Canadian, but it is restrained and not noisy. Every greeting the newcomer speaks is noted, every brief inquiry he makes (whom he mentions, whom he omits) carries the message from 'Ain ad-Dayr to them. One man's young son was missing from the welcomers; he was not standing by his father; even though the lad was only fourteen, he was not there. 'Adib asked; his asking was noted; it could be a shame to the father, and touched a whole community concern. I noted that all summer this was gently and persistently brought to bear upon all the Canadian-born youngsters: the obligations of their membership in the 'Ain ad-Dayr (and Druze) community. The intensity of the welcome for 'Abid was apparent to me as I listened to each exchange that he made with each and every wel-comer—handshake, kisses, the formal phrases, the swift and pointed query that activated bonds. 'Adib and all of us meeting with straight and quiet faces—the public sobriety of the Druzes, but activating a network of kinship that encompassed, eventually, all people of 'Ain ad-Dayr, at least. At one point he turned to me, too, with the proper quite salutation.

We were stared at by onlookers and the security men; it would be puzzling, perhaps, that so many people should meet one young man so gravely, so quietly, but with such customs of handshaking, embracing and kissing. Quickly the group broke up, dispersed. A few nights later 'Adib ate with us in a private home and the laughter and jokes and stories brought the inside of life in 'Ain ad-Dayr back and 'Adib as I "really" had known him.[5]

2. *'Ain ad-Dayr homes in Canada:* I visited a few, but not all of the homes in the Canadian city of 'Ain ad-Dayr people during the summer of 1966. Time was pressing and in selecting what I might best do in a limited period, I concentrated upon the stores that 'Ain ad-Dayr families were managing. Nevertheless, the half dozen homes I had time to visit give important insights into the reconstitution of 'Ain ad-Dayr life.

Although some villagers lived in the same neighborhoods, there was not, in 1966, any conspicuous clustering of the 'Ain ad-Dayr families in a colony or localized area. Choice of residence seemed to be determined rather by economic factors. One other point—no one lived in crowded "inner city" accomodations or large apartment houses. The dwellings are used in the same fashion as in 'Ain ad-Dayr, so far as Canadian construction allows, and this cuts very close to the heart of interpersonal habits, and style of life: furniture is arranged so that if one knows 'Ain ad-Dayr, one knows how to enter and where to sit down as a guest familiar in the community (everyone in Canada "knew all about" me, even though some of us had never met before). Some houses were used by two families and perhaps had been selected because their construction provided a central hall with rooms on each side, that allowed a close approximation of the way two families use a single building in 'Ain ad-Dayr. We drank maté[6], rather than tea, and my visits were concluded with Turkish coffee and candies. The lives of the women are eased by household appliances, and in some cases are more boring because there is less to do, but many of them work in factories, as char women, or as *de facto* managers of the stores which their husbands officially manage. Most of those I visited were eager to hear my version of a number of events that had occurred in 'Ain ad-Dayr in 1964-65—for the women's side compliments the men's. All expressed some wish that their mothers or sisters might be nearer—such are their lines of cooperation—and all seemed to hold aloof from their neighbors. All but the newcomers were speaking English with some ease—they learned it from television!

3. *Community gathering:* on the occasion of gathering as many of the 'Ain ad-Dayr community who wished to see the slides I had taken of 'Ain ad-Dayr in the year and a half I had spent in the village (1964-65), a community hall was engaged. The occasion was organized by several men of the "clan" I had resided with in 'Ain ad-Dayr. More than half the 'Ain ad-Dayr people in the city came (over a hundred), including families of both factions. All representatives in the city of the *mashayx* or gentry families were there, including the son of the religious *shayx* in 'Ain ad-Dayr. With him that evening I continued a long discussion of Platonic philosophy and contemporary science which we had begun the year before in Lebanon. Besides the showing of the slides, there was singing and dancing and refreshments. The climax of the evening was, perhaps, a half hour of the great circle dance of the *dabke*, a community dance of the Levant in which virtually all those present participated. During that time, as well as for the whole evening, the 'Ain ad-Dayr community was "reconstituted."

This seems, perhaps, an "artificial" occasion, a kind of special celebration or *hafli* for a special guest, such as I had seen, however, in the home village. However, on the occasions of weddings in Canada, similar gatherings are held. This evening, once again, all of the nuances of the Druze etiquette took place; I conveyed messages to people that I had been requested to do; I answered questions about delicate family concerns to this woman and that, carrying on the role that women often hold as transmitters of internal matters of concern, from my position as a quasi-member of one family. I had also, of course, to parry gently some questions as a matter of proper etiquette even though we all knew the answers.

Among those viewing the slides was the "oldest" immigrant to Canada from 'Ain ad-Dayr. At the age of ten he had come, about 1909, with an uncle. Three times he had returned to marry an 'Ain ad-Dayr girl, but the last occasion had been about 1948. A retired and prosperous farmer, he recalled taking his father's goats over the hills, but the shape of 'Ain ad-Dayr from the slides of 1964-65 amazed him: trees, gardens, and mansions he did not remember.

Concluding Remarks

The first point that should be conspicuous in this discussion is that the networks, segments, styles, manners and customs of the people of 'Ain ad-Dayr as a Lebanese village continue to flourish in a western Canadian city, and that economic, social, and ideological functions of greater security for all are so enhanced. The 'Ain ad-Dayr people live in Canadian houses, work in the Canadian economy, pay Canadian Taxes, hold Canadian citizenship, and the youngsters attend Canadian schools. A more extensive study would show some few occasions of conflict with the Canadian "system,"[7] but to a very remarkable degree the village of 'Ain ad-Dayr is successfully reconstituted in a Canadian city without friction, almost invisibly, unless one has been a member of it, by almost no more than a change of costume in public.

A second point that seems equally important to me is that while 'Ain ad-Dayr is a homeland location for its present living generations, the 'real' boundaries of the village are fixed in Lebanon only territorially and ideologically and not economically or socially. The strength of Druze identification, ideology (even among the essentially uninstructed), and kinship and the advantages of maintaining such solidarity seem to override deep assimilation or complete acculturation. There is, so far as I have been able to discover, very little erosion from the community. Even in the exceptionally high stress years after 1967, continuity is strong.

Explaining how this comes about does not fall to very quick analysis. To cite the mere prestige of success when a man retires to the village is not enough: he and his family acquire status which they could not enjoy (if they wanted it) in Canada, perhaps. All of the important symbols of Druze membership will be there— including the importance of consecrated funeral—and the powerful rules of Druze endogamy. These are effective factors.

But these preindustrial bonds survive because they have no competitive or counteractive mechanisms in the Canadian system: it is the latter system which can provide "nothing better." In fact, the weaknesses of the Canadian system—corporate industrialism with a denigrating class system which downgrades those without the proper Canadian British language, or skills, or education, or economic resources, and so inhibits movement out of the lowest levels of the working class, invites no one to give up his close family and clan life for the industrial alternatives: vagrancy and welfare. The flimsiness of industrial society for the individual or small group, on the one hand, and its *very* large-scale netting as a nation-state, leaves many gaps in which traditional village systems continue to function for the common security.

It is only the few very wealthy who will leave the 'Ain ad-Dayr community, whether in Canada or Lebanon, but even the few of these whom I know continue to show some of that Middle Eastern reaction of "shame."

NOTES

[1]Spontaneous" in the sense that no external planning or recruiting institution is now explicitly visible, such as the state immigration and settlement planning in Israel or the state or corporation recruiting of 19th and early 20th century Canada.

[3]This paper is concerned with the Canadian—'Ain ad-Dayr community continuity because, from observation, I know both ends. However, from my familiarity with 'Ain ad-Dayr there is a similar, but not as strong, continuity between 'Ain ad-Dayr and some locations in Latin America where similar but smaller groups of families are located. The differences are interesting in themselves but are not relevant here.

[4]All 'Ain ad-Dayr people seemed to be more knowledgable of the entrance regulations of all Western nations than officials themselves. In fact, their command of these legalities was remarkable and was used skillfully and patiently to maintain their traditional social groupings. Thus: A and B are brothers. A is a very prosperous merchant in a South American city. His wife and sons and daughters are in 'Ain ad-Dayr. B, a prospering businessman in Canada, needs help and, as would be customary, wishes to bring his nephew to help him and to participate. Although he has married several women of 'Ain ad-Dayr, he has no children. Because of the narrow nuclear family definition of Canadian immigration rules he cannot sponsor his nephew; he can sponsor his brother. His very wealthy brother comes from South America, under the proper legal documents, and establishes his residence in Canada. In due time he can sponsor his own son into Canada, which he does. The young man goes to work, as planned, with his uncle, and his father returns to his own business in South America. It may take two or three years of patient planning and execution, but it is done.

[5]Fortuitously, three years later, I arrived in the same terminal from Lebanon, and walked into a similar welcoming group from 'Ain ad-Dayr who were awaiting, unbeknownst to me, the arrival of another plane, of an older woman from 'Ain ad-Dayr. One member of the family I had lived with came forward at once and I explained to him why I had come very briefly, and then we all greeted each other quietly, with restraint, and I was only shamed that I could not remember every name. Needless to say, the university representative who was there to meet me stood aside in some amazement. In 1972 when I visited the family again, they retold the story of the encounter in every detail.

[6]*Maté*, an herb tea, brought from Brazil and Argentina, prevails as the social drink in the mountain villages of the Druze peasants, especially in the Anti-

Lebanon area. The gourd, silver tube, and other accoutrements are all present in the ceremony in ʿAin ad-Dayr as in Canada.

⁷Familial and factional conflicts have occasionally, but inadvertently, come afoul of Canadian law by misinterpretation of ʿAin ad-Dayr behavior. By and large, the ʾAin ad-Dayr community seeks a peaceful existence and avoids "breaking laws."

ᶻAin ad-Dayr is a pseudonym for the actual name of the village. See also Sweet 1967, 1968, 1969.

REFERENCES CITED

Abu-Lughod, J.
  1961   "Migrant Adjustment to City Life: The Egyptian Case."
          American Journal of Sociology 47:22-32.

Doughty, P.
  1970   "Behind the Back of the City: 'Provincial Life' in Lima, Peru."
          In W. Mangin 1970:30-46.

Mangin, W., editor
  1970   *Peasants in Cities: Readings in the Anthropology of Urbaniza-
          tion.* Boston: Houghton Mifflin Co.

Potter, J., M. Diaz, and G. Foster, editors
  1967   *Peasant Society: A Reader.* Boston: Little, Brown.

Sweet, L.E.
  1969   "Child's Play for the Ethnographer." *Behavior Science Notes*
          4:237-245.

  1967   "The Women of ʿAin ad-Dayr." *Anthropological Quarterly*
          40:167-183.

The Southeast Dearborn Arab Community Struggles for Survival Against Urban "Renewal"

BARBARA C. ASWAD[1]

In the southeastern section of Dearborn, Michigan, a community of approximately five thousand people, of which over half is of Arab cultural descent, has been presented with the problem of its continued existence in the face of the city's attempts to rezone the area from residential to heavy industry. The total community is referred to locally as the "South End", and will be referred to as such in this study. It is a low to middle income working class community and the majority of its members are immigrants. The Arab population is Muslim and the lands of their origin are Lebanon, Yeman, Palestine and Syria. Many are recent immigrants as we see in the fact that one third of the immigrants have lived in the U.S. and in this region five years or less.

The fact that these Middle Easterners are Muslims makes them a minority among the Arabic-speaking community in Detroit and the U.S. Of about 70,000 persons of Middle Eastern Arab background in Detroit, an approximate 10% are Muslims. The same ratio is true for the U.S. population of approximately one and one-half million. This community in Southeast Dearborn is probably the largest concentrated Arab Muslim community in the U.S.

In this essay, the author intends to portray several aspects of the community's struggle. First the following propositions will be investigated; one, that it is a primary community, that is one in

53

which relationships of kinship, friendship, and neighborliness are close, and one in which there are many local institutions which are frequently used by the community. Second that the majority of people have positive feelings toward the area, that they identify with it and desire to remain there. Third, that they will suffer if the community is destroyed, and fourth, that the present action being taken against the community is a case of class dominance and exploitation. We will also discuss the nature of the community and the political dialogue between the city and the community, (the most recent aspect of which is a class action suit filed against the city by the community.) These last two items cannot be separated totally in our discussion because they are not separated in reality. The community's planned removal seems in large part to be due to what the community is, as well as where it is located. Likewise, part of the organization of the community reflects attempts of the city to remove it.

Social and Historical Background of the Community

To effectively describe and evaluate the present situation, both politically and socially, one must highlight some of the historical happenings that have led to the current problems now facing the community.

The City of Dearborn is located within the Detroit metropolitan area. It is bounded on three sides by the city of Detroit. It is the center of the industrial and administrative functions of the huge Ford Motor Company. Located within the city is not only the world headquarters of the corporation, but also its largest industrial facility, indeed one of the largest if not the largest single industrial complexes in the world, the Rouge complex. One of the primary attendant problems of the plant is pollution. Two years ago the Wayne County Anti-Pollution Division of the Wayne County Health Department set the level of fallout of the suspended particulate matter spewed into the air by this facility at 220 tons per square mile per year.[2] This by-product of auto manufacturing has created the most densely polluted air in the Detroit region, one of the most highly industrialized areas in the country and the world.

The facility has also attracted to the area a diversified combination of ethnic groups. The Rouge began its initial development in the early 1920's when Ford expanded its facilities from their original plant in Highland Park, a small city in the center of the city of Detroit. Immigrant groups, primarily from central and southern Europe were imported in great numbers to man the fast-growing industrial centers. Many of those employed in the Highland Park Plant moved to the Rouge Plant. The immigrants settled as close to this installation in Dearborn as possible, initially to be able to walk to work, later because there were already relatives and members of their own ethnic group living there. They thus became a supply of abundant, cheap labor. As business expanded, news of jobs spread and relatives from abroad, or U.S. citizens from the southern U.S. would come to seek employment. If business decreased and there were layoffs, some might migrate back, some would tighten their belts or seek aid from their relatives.

Concurrently, conditions of uncertainty, war, or poverty in the homelands of the immigrants propelled certain waves into these centers. Examples include the early Polish and Italian immigrants, and most recently the Palestinians and Southern Lebanese, the latter two groups having experienced Israeli occupation or incursion into their villages.

Overlaying these push-pull conditions, were the U.S. Government immigration rules. Relatives have often had first priority in these rules, as they do now in the 1970s. Thus we find the communities highly characterized by groups of relatives, and persons from the same villages and areas. Refugees have also been given special status in immigration laws and this affects the character of community composition. Through the 1920s and into the 1940s, the South End was composed largely of Italian, Rumanian and Polish groups. The Arabic speaking population was small at these times, but grew larger in the period from the late 1940s to the present time.

It was mentioned in the introduction to this volume, that various ethnic communities in Detroit have moved along different street corridors into the suburbs in the last twenty years and that they formed secondary ethnic communities in the suburbs. This movement divided the Arabic speaking communities primarily according to their diverse religious and geographical origins in the Middle East, so that the Lebanese Maronites live in the eastern suburbs, the Iraqi Chaldeans in the northern suburbs and so forth. A rise in their socio-economic standards accompanied these movements, and usually the urban center was not maintained. Persons have also left the South End, however it has remained an area which has continuously received immigrants and it is the only Middle Eastern community in the Detroit area whose members are primarily of the unskilled laboring class. [3]

Another facet of history which affected the South End community occurred during the late 1930s and early 1940s when the attempts to organize the Ford Motor Co. under the United Auto Workers began. The South End community constituted the largest and most powerful voting block in the City of Dearborn. Many of the union organizers and members were residents of the Southend. Union organization activities were not confined solely to shop activities but were openly and actively carried out in the community. Conflicts soon arose as to whether to organize or not. Relatives were pitted against relatives, but the decision to organize grew more popular and prevalent. At that time, Henry Ford I hired as his right hand man and head of the infamous "goon" squad, Harry Bennett. Many of his henchmen, were residents of the South End.

Today, the Ford Motor Co., earns more profit each year than the national budgets of most of the countries from which the people living in the South End have migrated. [4] The other areas of Dearborn, the middle class and the more affluent areas, have expanded greatly over the last thirty years leaving the South End in a weakened political position. It is currently very much an area "on the other side of the tracks." Yet it still functions as an area in which immigrants come to work in the factories.

To the outsider who talks or drives through the area today, several things are immediately obvious. It is adjacent to the Rouge plant and the Levy Asphalt Co. on two sides, on the other sides a cemetary, a park and railroad tracks bound the community so that it is geographically an enclave. On its eastern side beyond the cemetary and park are the Detroit city limits and some persons of western Dearborn tend to think of the area as belonging to Detroit. The houses are of varying styles, most are of frame, brick or stucco in the thirty and forty year age bracket. They are primarily one or

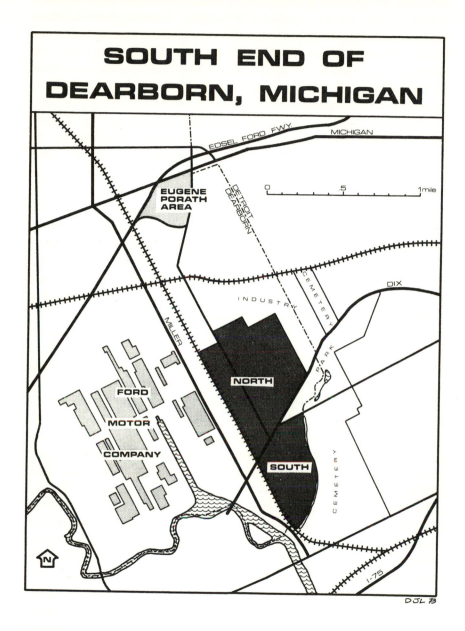

SOUTH END OF DEARBORN, MICHIGAN

two family houses. Most have neat lawns and many have gardens. There are also a few multiple dwellings. Commercial establishments consisting largely of Middle Eastern restaurants and coffee houses, small grocery stores and other small businesses line Dix Road, a road which serves as a north-south division for the community (see map). Of course one sees and smells the billowing and polluting fumes. Along with the general nature of housing, one sees that the majority of the inhabitants are of the working class and are of the middle and lower middle income bracket. The median income for the area was $8,006 for families and unrelated individuals in the 1970 Census (1970;251). This compares with a median for Dearborn of $11,429 (ibid:227). In Dearborn 7.9% of all households are listed below the poverty level in the census while 21.3% of the South End are in this category (ibid:227, 251).[5] Unemployment is 9% in the South End compared to 2.4% for Dearborn as a whole (ibid: 156, 176). Put in another way, the area constitutes 5% of the population of the city yet accounts for 14% of all the families below the poverty level and 13% of the city's unemployed. Also, most of these unemployed cannot be accounted for as elder citizens in the South End. Only 18.4% of this category in the South End are 65 years and older while for Dearborn, the same percent is 31.6% (ibid: 175, 152). The area has 16% of the families in Dearborn that are on welfare, and only 3% of these are living on social security.

This other part of the South End's environment, that is, the rest of the residential area of Dearborn, is not as visable to the outside observer, since the South End is physically separated from that part of Dearborn by numerous railroad tracks, a major freeway, and the Ford Rouge plant itself. The seventh largest city in Michigan with 103,000 persons, Dearborn has one of the highest annual budgets. Fifty three percent of the city's taxes are paid for by Ford Motor Co. (City of Dearborn 1970:5). This allows low property taxes and numerous benefits for the city's residents. The city has achieved a national reputation as an all-white working class city, although its all-white, anti-Black reputation outweights the other reputation. It is hardly less integrated than most of the other areas bordering Detroit, however, it has earned its fame due to its pompous and highly verbal mayor of thirty years, Orville Hubbard, and the outstanding fact that many of the workers who contribute to Ford's fortunes are

Black (perhaps as high as 50%), yet they cannot live in the City to reap the tax benefits.

In the above discussion, we have tried to indicate the intimate relationship between the Ford Motor Co., the City of Dearborn and the South End. Such communities as the South End are not divorced enclaves in a city, they are very much part of the whole urban industrial complex which is part of a larger worldwide phenonema of migration and the supply of cheap labor.[6]

Today, another characteristic which is immediately visable to the outsider and which gives the South End its unique quality, is its Middle Eastern flavor. The coffee shops with men standing around the entrances, the Islamic Mosque with Middle Eastern architecture, the many signs in Arabic, and swarthy appearance of the people and the frequency with which Arabic is heard, all tell the observer that the core of this community is from the Mid-East and that many are recent migrants.

As in many immigrant communities, the core of the population is from one region, but numerous other groups are represented. We have noted how that core has changed in the fifty years. It is interesting to note that some of those of Arabic background, particularly those from Yeman would be classified as darker than many Detroit Blacks on a skin color pigmentation scale. Perhaps it is their foreign extraction and their physical separation from the rest of the city that has allowed this community to survive in Dearborn even this long. On the other hand, it may be a factor contributing to the current position of the city. We also mentioned the factor of the dropping population in the area over the past 50 years, and the associated diminished importance the area has in voting.

One visable characteristic of the area reflects the struggle itself, although the outsider might not understand the implications of numerous scattered vacant lots, of whole blocks with no houses on them, a growing number of playgrounds and parking lots, and numerous unrepaired homes. The decision of the city nearly 20 years ago to rezone the area to heavy industry has resulted in this appearance. Some of the measures which have aided this process are mentioned later.

Most of the above items are fairly visable to the outsider. What is

not so immediately visable are the feelings of the inhabitants of ap-
preciation of their community and its spirit, of their apprehension
and anxiety over the future of their homes and lives, of feelings of
suspicion, of division and of unity created by this threat, of
wondering whether they should get out while they can (if they
can), and of anger. The visability of these feelings became manifest
in the organization by some members of the community into the
Southeast Dearborn Community Council (SEDCC).

The Council, which is discussed later, organized demonstrations,
clean-up campaigns and most recently engaged the City in a legal
suit before a Federal Court. Other members of the community wait
to see who will emerge the victor, the City or the community.

A number of other studies have been done on various aspects of
this community. Elkholy's study (1966) compares this community
to Toledo's Muslim community, Wasfi's unpublished dissertation
(1964) analyzes the social organization, particularly marriage patterns, of the Lebanese in the community, and Wigle's essay in this
volume discusses a number of the social characteristics of the community. In order not to be repetitious, we will limit this essay to
a discussion of the factors which seem important to the question of
the disruption of the community. One of the major sources of our
study is a survey conducted by the author in the early fall of 1971
(Aswad 1973). The survey sampled the total community and included 180 households.[7] Blocks were selected randomly with adjustments made to account for differences in population
concentration.[8] Ten students served as interviewers. These included graduate and undergraduate students in anthropology at
Wayne State University and one South End student. Four of the
students were Arabic speakers and three others had had Arabic
courses at the University.

Social Characteristics of the Community
Background, Occupation and Education

The vast majority (86%) of the Arab community in the Southend
was born abroad and is from villages. In the processes of rural-
urban migration, we find communities forming in the city which
reflect the social institutions, mores and customs of the regions
from which the migrants come. This occurs in cases of migration

within a country, as Abu-Lughod (1961) had demonstrated in Egypt, as well as in international migration. The ties to the villages are also strengthened by frequent trips or migration of certain members back to the village of origin. Thus information networks are kept open.

The nature of the social organization is characterized by close primary ties, that is with kinsmen, villagers, neighbors and friends. For many, these social networks are also economic networks in which migrants depend upon one another for help in obtaining jobs, sharing of food and engaging in reciprocal relations which provide help and security in unfavorable times. These close relationships are seen not only as a carry over from the areas from which they migrated, but also as a mode of adaptation to the new situation in a complex urban environment. This environment is one in which they usually lack the necessary job skills, education and language to adapt easily at first.

The type of social groups formed depends in part upon the type of migration pattern engaged in. For example, in the Lebanese community, we find some families that have been here for fifty years and consequently there are numerous members of the second and third generations and a young forth generation in the community. Many of the original members intended to make money and return home. Some did, but others found themselves bound in the conditions of having a family and high living expenses in the U.S.. Few had good economic alternatives in the home country or village. Inheritance often played an important part, and disputes are reported whereby the persons in the home village wanted to buy the migrant's share of inheritance. Large amounts of money were often sent to relatives in the village either to keep their inheritance or to obtain brides. Over the years they have brought relatives and wives into the community and continue to do so. In some cases, immigrants have migrated from Lebanon to West Africa and then to the South End. Currently the Lebanese and their descendants constitute 46.8% of the Arab population in the area and 24.4% of the total South End population. The recent inexpensive international charter airflights have increased the interaction between the communities. Also the recent Israeli bombings, and incursions into their villages has brought great grief and anxiety to this population and it would seem that this pressure will result in further migration to the South End.[9]

One of the most obvious cases of the process of chain migration of relatives from one village is that of Tibnine. There are approximately 400-600 persons from this village living within about 5 blocks of each other. Many members live in one of two apartment houses which are owned by other persons from the village. Wasfi reports that there are five major patrilineages in the area and 400 members from one patrilineage, the Berry patrilineage, living in the South End (1966:108). All of the Southern Lebanese in the South End are members of the Imami Shia sect of Islam.

The Lebanese aided their relatives and also provided assistance to the Yemani and Palestinian immigrants. The Yemani population has a few members who have been in the Detroit region some 40 years, but the majority of the group has migrated in the last twenty years or so. Their pattern of migration differs significantly from that of the Lebanese, and is what Gonzales refers to as "recurrent migration" (1961). This is characterized as: "in recurrent migration men make irregular journeys, of varying lengths of time, to obtain wage labor throughout their productive years." (1961:1268) There are few Yemani families in this community. Rather there are numerous single men and men whose families remain in Yeman. Many members return to their country to join their families. (This is due in part to laws in Yeman which have made it difficult for women to come to the U.S. These laws are currently being modified.)

While most of the Lebanese own homes, the Yemanis primarily are renters and live together in some of the hotels or multiple dwelling units, or rent rooms in houses with other Yemanis. As is common with the majority of the workers in the community, most Yemanis work in the auto factories, however a number also work on ships. Many have also worked as fruit and vegetable pickers, primarily in California. It seems that their historical association with working on ships has given them the mobility associated with recurrent migratory practices and has allowed them to return home and invest their capital. The villagers are from several villages in the southeast North Yeman, in a mountain region around Rishaya. They are of the Zaidi Shia sect of Islam. Some of the northerners lived in the cities of South Yeman before migrating, others come directly from the villages. Other Yemani are from the cities of the South originally and are of the Sunni sect of Islam. The whole community has a very strong association called the Yemani Benevolent Association. They have their own club unit which serves both as a coffee house and a club house.

The third Arab group, the Palestinians, represent a relatively new group. They came in waves after the two major wars and occupations of their land by Zionists. That is, after the 1948 war and after the 1967 war. Recently there is a new influx from occupied territories of the West Bank in what apears to be an agreement to reduce the population in that area by the governments of Israel and the U.S. Among the Palestinians we find patterns of family groups and of single men. In contrast to the Lebanese who have numerous relatives from their villages here, we find that there are a number of Palestinians who do not have many relatives in the South End. This may be due to their being scattered as refugees before migration as well as the forceful nature of their migration. There is one village however, that has supported a pattern of chain migration. The Palestinians are members of the Sunni sect of Islam.

One of the most important characteristics of this Middle Eastern community is the fact that ethnic and kinship ties are constantly being reinforced by the new immigrants. *One third* of the Arabic speaking population has lived in this country for *five years or less.* Some of the second and third generation members have moved from the area when they achieved a level of financial improvement, while others have invested in homes in the area. Due to this latter group there is a range of incomes in the South End,[10] and a variety of occupations. There are a couple of doctors and one professor who have bought homes there.

As we mentioned before, those who move out generally move to the neighboring western communities. Some come back to visit their kin frequently, and it is common to hear persons say that they miss their neighbors and the closeness of the community. Thus the area functions as one of acculturation, adjustment and socialization for new members as well as an area of permanent residence for many and a home base to return to for others.

Two-thirds of the Arab immigrants did not know English when

they arrived. The general level of education in the South End Arab community is as follows: 21.3% have had no formal education, 30.9% have had primary or secondary school education, 27.3% have attended high school and 18.5% have been to college. The last percentage represents primarily second and third generation members in the community.

The Salina school is an important institution of acculturation in the community and the people have pride in it. Most of the activities which are held as a whole community are housed there. Also the teachers have been sensitive to the needs of immigrant people. With an elementary population thirty-three percent foreign born and a junior high population eighteen percent foreign-born, the people of the community have given the teachers much credit for their special concern. Such things as substituting a protein diet when pork is served in the cafeteria is also appreciated. In the evenings, English classes for the foreign born are given at the school. When the Dearborn Board of Education decided to close the Salina school in 1970, the entire community rallied to stop this action. In 1971, the Board threatened to close English-language evening classes. Again the community acted to pressure this foreclosure of a major path of assimilation for new immigrants.

When asked what their previous jobs had been, 45% indicated that they had been engaged in agriculture in villages. Most considered themselves to have owned "medium" amounts of land rather than large or small amounts. None were of primarily share-cropping backgrounds. 13% said they had been workers, 3.3% had been merchants, 6.7% clerks, 3.3% skilled laborers, and the remainder were either too young, had been in school or are housewives.

Leeds has expressed in his studies of persons who have migrated to Brazilian "squatments" that these communities have wrongly been characterized as "rural enclaves" in an urban setting; that urbanization has spread to the countryside and many immigrants are therefore not unfamiliar with customs, work and attitudes of the urban sector (1967). Thus he feels that the urban-rural dicotomy is a false one. In our case there are two considerations which seem important in this regard. Leed's discussion primarily concerns rural workers on plantations, while in our discussion most of the rural workers have come from villages that have been partially subsistence oriented and partially mercantile oriented. Certainly until recently they have emphasized subsistence more than the Brazilian plantations and thus are closer to a peasant rather than worker category. Secondly they are migrating into a highly industralized urban center in a foreign country. Thus the differences in experiences, values and life styles would be greater in our example for those who come directly from the villages.

On the other hand we do find urban type experiences in the fact that some Yemani have previously worked on ships and other unskilled labor jobs, in the fact that there are close connections between most Lebanese villages and cities, and their villages are often the size of towns (Tibnine is several thousand persons). Also the Lebanese villager has had a long history of selling some of his products, and many times these included cash crops such as silk, apples, tobacco. He has also often had relatives who became merchants or workers in Africa, Latin America and the U.S. Contacts were kept between these societies, and thus the Lebanese villager had had merchantile experiences and urban and foreign connections greater than many Middle Eastern villagers.

Thus we should be cautioned against thinking of the area merely as an "urban village". It is, as we mentioned an integral part of the history of industralization in our country.

Currently three-fourths of the community have hourly jobs with over half working in the auto factories. Approximately one third of the community commutes to jobs in auto factories and other jobs in areas approximately forty minutes away from the South End. Thus many members have chosen the area to reside in for reasons other than the proximity of their jobs. [11]

Religion

As noted in the studies in this volume of the Christian Arab communities that came to Detroit, many attended established churches and some sent their children to church schools. But the Muslim community had to establish its own mosques. The first was established in 1926 in Highland Park (a city within the boundaries of Detroit) where the first Ford Motor Co. plant was located, then it moved to the South End Dearborn in 1924 when Ford establish its Rouge plant.

As we have seen different sects of Islam are represented, both the major Sunni and Shia sects, and two branches within the Shia. There are two mosques and a religious hall called the Hashimite Hall which serve the community. The local mosque is a Sunni mosque. The Shia attend the Islamic Center about a mile away, built on property bought from Ford and located next to the Episcopal Church in whose cemetary Henry Ford lies buried. These local religious institutions serve as places where men's and women's clubs meet and wedding receptions and funerals are held.

The factor of religion as well as kinship has obviously played a role in the community's attraction for new members. It is also the only major area of Muslim concentration in the Detroit area.[12] Most of the other Arab Muslims who live in the Detroit area attend the mosque outside the community, but also they sometimes attend functions at the local mosque. Thus the two mosques keep the two Muslim communities in touch with each other. The mosques are also now functioning as meeting places for Arabic associations whose membership is both Christian and Muslim and thus they are brought in touch to some degree with some other members of the Arab community. A few members of Detroit's Black Muslim community frequent the mosques, particularly the one in the South End, and thus there is some limited interaction between these ethnic groups, other than on the assembly lines.

We might also mention that in some of the assembly line disputes, there has been both agreement and antagonism between the Black and Arab communities. One major cause for antagonism is due to the fact that some workers from the Arab community will work for cheap wages, while Blacks are now active in organizing and demanding workers rights. At other times they have banded together.

Other Social Networks of the Arabs and other Members of the Community

For most members of the Arabic speaking communities of the South End, primary group networks of kinship, friendship and neighborhood overlap with much frequency. Again, the strongest example of this is seen by members of such villages as Tibnine which we mentioned previously. In our sample 65% of the Arabic sample responded that they came to the South End because they have kinsmen here. 66% said they came directly to this area from the Middle East, and 41% said that kinsmen helped them obtain their first jobs. A strong 85% said that they ate at least once a week with relatives other than their immediate family in the South End and 34% said they ate daily with such relatives. Fifty percent of those Arabs interviewed were married to their relatives. Relative marriage, particularly that with father's brother's daughter or other close relatives is a preferred marriage pattern in the Middle East and serves such functions as keeping property in tact for the patrilineal segment, and allowing the kin group to attain an efficient level of political and social corporateness. (See Aswad 1971:75-85 for a fuller analysis). In the case of immigrants, we see the marriage pattern reinforcing chain migration patterns and American immigration rules which favor entrance of close relatives.

We may note in the following figures the similarity among those of Arabic descendant and those of non-Arabic descent in their emphasis upon primary group relationships, but also note that Arabs emphasize kin relations more than the non-Arab sample, and show a higher response to primary group interaction in general. We shall indicate the question first then the Arab and non-Arab responses separately.

When asked what they liked about the South End area the most, the highest responses were 1) relatives live here (Arab=40%, Non-Arab=6%), 2) my neighbors (Arabs=13.8%, Non-Arab = 52.3%). To this question Arabs also indicated the cultural and linguistic character of the area (Arabs=21.3%, Non-Arabs=0.0%). Other items such as jobs, schools, low cost area, health, safety, were all below 10% in both groups.

When asked a question regarding what characteristics in a new area they would look for if they were to move, the answers were similar to those in the above paragraph with the only difference being that the non-Arab sample indicated neighbors less often and such items as schools, and the economic characteristics of the area to a higher extent.

Approximately half of the sample owns their homes, or is buying them. Half rent, and of those who rent, Arabs rent more from landlords within the area of the Southend, while non-Arabs tend to rent from landlords who live outside the area.

Both samples felt that parents should live near their families rather than in special homes when they are older, but again the Arab response was stronger. (Arab=83%, Non-Arab=54.7%). One third of the non-Arab group indicated preference for special homes, against 14.9% of the Arab sample.

Visiting is an important function in the Middle East, particularly among women. These visits serve to constantly reinforce or create primary kin and neighborhood relationships. They may also serve political functions. (see Aswad:1972) Similar functions are achieved among men through their frequenting coffee houses and clubs.[13] About half of the Arab sample indicated that they spent as high as 75%-100% of their leisure time visiting friends or relatives, or in the coffee houses and clubs *in the South End*. Of the non-Arab sample 39.4% indicated the same. In these same leisure activities outside the area, the response was that very few went outside. For example those indicating that they spent *no leisure time outside* the South End in visiting or club activities was Arab=64.9%, Non-Arab=40.7%. Another question intended to measure their community relationships asked if the majority of their friends lived in the South End or outside of it. 80% of the Arabs said inside, 46% of the Non-Arabs indicated the same.

Answers to other questions designed to measure interaction indicated that over half the Arab sample help each other care for each other's children during the week. This is particularly important for women who work, but is widespread in the community on a basis of reciprocity.

Feelings Toward the Area and Urban Renewal

The feelings of the vast majority interviewed are very positive toward the South End as an area in which to live. The guesto with which persons responded to these questions was noted by all the interviewers. Informants wanted to go far beyond the questions asked them and would start to expound on the nature of the good qualities of the community. Much of this is obviously genuine, and in addition it seems in part to be a response to the crisis level that the city's rezoning project had reached in threatening the community at the time of the interviewing.

Both samples indicated that they feel safer in the South End than they would either in Detroit or in the rest of Dearborn (Arab=95.7%, Non-Arab=84.9%). When they were asked why this was so, the following major reasons were: 1) I know people here (Arab=26.6%, Non-Arab=11.6%) 2) No crile in the area (Arab=10.6%, Non-Arab=24.4%), 3) Ethnic reasons (Arab =21.3%, Non-Arab=3.5%), 4) Cohesiveness of the community (Arab=12%, Non-Arab=15%), 5) Whites live here only (Arabs=3.2%, Non-Arab=15.1%). It was also often mentioned as an indication of their feelings of security that "People here often don't lock their doors, you can walk in and visit with your friends." We personally observed much of this frequent and open visiting and entering of one another's homes. It is reasonable to say that such a phenonema and feeling is somewhat rare in our urban centers today, certainly it is rare in the suburbs.

When asked about their feelings toward moving out of the area and the possibility of being forced to leave, by far the great majority said that *they do not want to leave the South End.* (Arab=79.8%, Non-Arab=67.4%, total sample 73.9%, indicated this). Of those who indicated that they would move, (23.8%) their primary reasons for moving were first, that the city will eventually take the area (34.7%). Secondly because of too much pollution (24.5%). Thirdly that they felt they could afford a better place (22.7%). On the other hand of this sample, only 1.5% said they wanted to move because they didn't like the community or people. These latter were all non-Arabs. Thus the indications showing the positive attitudes of both the Arab and Non-Arab sample are very strong, and of the small minority that would like to move from the area, the main reasons were pollution and the urban renewal program of the City.

When the people were asked if they felt the City was forcing them to move, we find a high positive response in both groups. (Arab = 55%, Non-Arab = 47.7%). In the non-Arab group there was also a high negative response (44.2%). Among the Arabs there was a significant number who did not respond (Negative = 28.7%, 21% = No Response).

From these questions and answers, we find that the people in the community do like the area very much and have been living here by choice, at least by choice within the confines of their economic positions. Thus when outsiders comment so easily "The area should be torn down, it is not good for the people" or "I don't know why people want to live on 30'-40' plots anyway," they are totally neglecting the people's own desires, needs and feelings toward the area. They are looking at "houses" instead of "homes," at "streets" which need repair instead of a "community" which exists. Indeed the people do not like the pollution, they are the ones who asked that the City to try to control the pollution.

Just as their feelings toward the community register positively, some of their feelings toward outsiders are characterized with feelings of distrust. The question on safety which we mentioned above is perhaps most significant here. We also asked a question of whether they felt they would be discriminated against in other regions. The replies were as follows: "Yes strongly" (Arabs 25.5%, Non-Arab 7%) "Yes medium" (Arab = 14.8%, Non-Arab = 9.3%) "Yes weak" (Arab = 7.4%, Non-Arab = 8.1%). All answering "Yes" (Arab = 47.8%, Non-Arab = 24.4%). Those answering "No" were (Arab = 38.3%, Non-Arab 59.3%). It was obvious that the Arabs felt this potential discrimination more strongly than non-Arab groups. When the Arabs were asked why this would be, 79.5% of those who indicated yes said it would be for ethnic reasons, (being an Arab), about half of the non-Arab sample indicated ethnic reasons. The other major reasons were religion and socio-economic class in that order.

When the Arab sample was asked if they felt the U. S. newspapers were fair in their presentation of the Middle Eastern situation, two thirds of those who answered said no and two-thirds said they felt that their culture is not presented accurately in the U. S. On these two questions, a high percentage refused to answer the questions.

Community Versus the City: Renewal or Removal History
In 1953 the Dearborn City Planning Commission decided to reevalute the use of the South End from residential to some use more suitable for the City, namely rezoning the area to heavy industry. At this time a community organization was formed and it approached the City Planning Commission. The community organization opposed any rezoning to heavy industry and they argued that they would like the City to improve the environment and make

it a better residential area. The arguments on each side are essentially the same today. Since the early 1950s the City sponsored numerous projects, one has had federal funding through HUD, the others have been City funded. In a Trial Brief of a class action suit brought against the City by the community organization in 1971, the projects were described:

> "None have had meaningful citizen participation; some have had no real City Council participation. All have involved the accomplished or planned removal of all residences to be replaced by business and industry. None have involved the building of new housing (Other than a grand total of two homes on Riverside that are mentioned repeatedly by the City for each project) and none have involved serious relocation efforts on the part of the City. All have taken place without formal condemnation, with the exception of three lots in one federally-assisted project." (Amen et. al. v. The City of Dearborn et. al. 1973a:8)

Between 1960 and 1970, the U.S. census shows that there was a 25% reduction of dwellings in the area. During the last approximate ten years, the City has acquired 356 lots. (Ibid: 1973b:12) This was accomplished primarily through two projects. One was financed by HUD. It was begun in 1962, 85 families were displaced and the area sold to the Levy Co., a company that uses Ford slag to make asphalt and to Mercier, a brick manufacturer. They occupied the cleared regions in 1968. In 1966, 92 families were displaced and the area sold to Ford Leasing Development Company, a subsidary of Ford Motor Co. These projects all used land in the northern section of the community.

The increased pollution from the industralization of these residential areas was evident to the people in the northern section. Their streets had clay on them, heavy tandem trucks thundered down residential streets spilling bricks, slag piles sometimes grew up to sixty feet and some slag began to spill into residents' backyards. The community organization was reorganized and called the South East Dearborn Community Council (SEDCC). The City meanwhile used the increased pollution from these industries as a reason for requesting addition funds to clear adjoining residential areas that they said were now no longer fit to be residential areas. "These projects were designed to move down the South End slowly one street at a time in a phased destruction of the entire area", according to the plaintiffs. (Ibid 1973a; 40).

Also during the 1960's there was discussion of a new housing and office complex that was to be built by Ford Motor Co. on Ford property in central Dearborn. There were rumors in the community that low income housing would be included and available to members of the South End. When the multimillion dollar Fairlane Project plans finally emerged (in the late 1960s and early 1970s), it was evident that the housing was designed for those of upper incomes.

The frequent shifting of clearance boundaries by the City Planning Committee led to much confusion, uncertainty and division in the community. Since 1962, nine different renewal projects have been proposed in the section north of Dix Road, many of them had overlapping boundaries. (See Ibid: 1973a:13-33) The City was denied the additional Federal funding which they had requested but proceded with their own funding. Part of their plan included dividing the community at Dix Road and indicating that the southern section of the community was a "conservation area," not a "clearance area". This had the effect of dividing the community, with the southern section (the major area of the Arab concentration) sitting back hoping they would not be touched. In the final summation of the law suit however, it was interesting to observe that the City lawyer designated the entire South End as an "anachronism" in a "sea of industry." Obviously if the northern section were rezoned industrial, and particularly if the school were lost, the southern section would become even more of an "anachronism" in the eyes of the City.

The SEDCC brought their classification suit against the City in 1971.[14] They were represented in the case by the Center for Urban Law and Housing, a division of Wayne County Neighborhood Legal Services which is sponsored by the Office of Economic Opportunity. A temporary restraining order was placed on the City in 1972 ordering them to refrain from actively purchasing homes and forbiding them from rezoning untill a decision in the case was reached. During this period, however, the City managed to purchase approximately 40 additional homes, using a clause of the restraining order which allowed them to purchase homes in case of owner hardship. (Ibid. 1973b:4-5).

In August 1973, an opinion was given by the judge in favor of the community. In a 36 page statement, he found "That the City and its officials had taken the plaintiffs' property without due process of law." Among the thirty-three allegations brought against the City, he agreed with twenty-eight. He found that Dearborn "forced people to sell to the city" by denying or delaying building permits, requiring residents to perform maintenance or install items not required by the City building code, discouraging repairs, leaving City-owned vacant lots in an unsightly and unkept state. He said that the private market in the area was destroyed by announcements from City officials that FHA insurance was unavailable in the areas, by repeated announcements that the two areas are being cleared, and by posting signs throughout the area urging residents to sell to the City. (Ibid:1973b)

In some cases, the judge found that the City had allowed its properties in the area to remain unprotected and posted signs reading "Free at your risk. Take any part of the house, Hurry." He also ruled that the City had contributed to pollution by selling property to "A large processor of asphalt, and a brick manufacturer". He ruled that the City "Has not been offering fair compensation to the home owners" in the areas. He stated that the City did not follow two state laws which required the city to develop a relocation plan for persons displaced by the clearance and to set up a district council to allow local citizens to participate in decisions affecting their areas. He enjoined the City from acquiring any additional property in the areas, denying building or repair permits for homes in the areas, posting signs, soliciting sales and engaging in other acts designed to encourage sales, and he forbade zoning changes for five years. He gave the 350 displaced homeowners the opportunity to sue the City.

His decision however allowed the City to purchase "substandard" properties and that definition was subject to negotiation with the City. The City may also go ahead with its clearance project if it abides by federal and state laws. (Principally the Federal Blighted Areas Act and a Michigan Relocation Act).

Thus the community and the City are now in for more confrontations and while it gives the community some breathing time, it means "The beginning of a new struggle to rehabilitate the South End" according to the President of SEDCC, Al Amen. One attorney said that the findings were "really a good catalogue of what happens in urban renewal—how people suffer. The people that are left are really going to have to organize and fight . . . . to save that area". The City, meanwhile, is contemplating an appeal of the case. Thus, we may conclude that the struggle must now be carried out legally by the city, but we may guess that it is not over for the residents.

Divisions within the Community and Relation
of the Divisions to City pressures

There are numerous divisions within the community. Some of the most obvious are geographical, those north of Dix road and south of Dix Road. This division coincides to a high extent with the Arab, Non-Arab majorities. (Arabs South of Dix Road = 73.5%, North of Dix Road 26.5%; Non-Arabs, South 34.4%, North 61.6%.) This division therefore also coincides generally with the Muslim Christian division. Since the Arab community has more newcomers in it, we will also find more newcomers in the south and older residents in the north. As we've shown the city is primarily attempting to rezone the northern section, and has at times, including the present, told the south that it will remain as it is.

There are divisions between home owners and renters. Many of the latter are newcomers, and we find the home owners of the northern section to be those most directly involved and most active in the Southeast Community Council. Of course newcomers can be directly threatened by their alien status. In a community with such close kin ties, the extention of this threat to relatives can have an affect of immobilizing a large segment of the community.

There are many social divisions in the community such as those between families and single men, those between persons from different regions and village within those regions, those between different ethnic groups, those who have come directly from a village, or those who have been to urban areas before migration. All these in some way affect reactions to the divide and rule policies of the City at some time.

The most active members of the community on the SEDCC are among the following: These from the northern segment who are immediately threatened, older immigrants who own homes, again primarily from the north. Of the Arab population, it is those who live in the north and primarily married women and younger men of the 2nd and 3rd generations. From my observation, the leaders of the large Arab kin groups and other associations have not been active. Most of them do not live in the north and they seem to be waiting to see who emerges the victor, the City or the Council. It might be added that one of the most influential and constant factors in the SEDCC is a school teacher who lives outside of the South End but has taught in the school thirty five years, and is active in party politics at the local and state levels.

One effect of the court case is worth noting. Previous to the Council's court action, there was some noticeable action on the part of the community organization. Pickets were formed, members were able to assemble several hundred members of the community to attend City Council meetings in protest. It appears to the author that the lengthy procedures of the court (2-1/2 years) plus the ability of the City to continue buying homes during the period of the restraining order, demoralized the community as they saw their residential area shrinking.

Thus while some led the struggle to the courts, others weighed their strategies, and many engaged in a sort of helpless unreality of the sort typified by "it can't happen to us". The latter attitude is reminiscent of the history of the Boston Westend community and its inability to react in the face of its destruction, as told by Herbert Gans in the *Urban Villagers* (1961). Without the efforts of the Neighborhood Legal Services, the Boston story would undoubtedly have been repeated in an almost identical fashion here. It is too early to evaluate their reactions to the case, but many members seem amazed that they won.

The relation of other Arabic speaking communities in the Detroit region to this situation has been general inactivity and lack of knowledge. The communities are separated by many factors, geography, infrequent social communication, socio-economic class distinctions, and their historical separateness, which has often involved rivalry and even hostility in the home countries. Some members of the Association of Arab-American Graduates (AAUG) and other organizations have made an attempt to aid the group, but for the most part it has been as individuals rather than as associations.[15] One may ask, what is the reaction by members who have moved out of the South End to higher income areas. It is mixed, but many react with the "we made it" syndrome so common among those of upward mobility, forgetting in many cases what contributed to their process of achievement, or forgetting that the displaced persons are being given no reasonable alternatives. Their secure homes, income levels and knowledge of English allow many to say "That terrible polluted place should be torn down anyway" without much thought for who is to bear the sacrifices. There is also enough changeover in ethnic composition that some have said "Well the place has changed . . . when I lived there there there weren't so many . . . etc."

Thus we may say that there are divisions with the community, as there are in any community, and the City has managed to aggravate many of these by the pressures for rezoning.

Effects of Destruction of Community

What are the effects of destruction of community and the dislocation of people. In the Boston Westend area, Fried found that it was:

> "Likely to increase social and psychological "pathology" in some cases, new opportunities in some, and increase the rate of social mobility for others but for the greatest number, neither pathology nor mobility resulted but an intense personal suffering despite a moderately successful adaptation in relocation" (1963:167)

He reported that it caused a fragmentation of their sense of spatial identity, group identity and a shattering of feelings of security. The dislocation created a loss of residential area identification which had provided a sense of continuity, important in many working class cultures (ibid:157). He also found that the stronger the person's pre-location commitment to the area, the more likely he is to react with marked grief (ibid:154).

We have many other studies of immigrant groups to know that the initial impact of immigration is overwhelming. It is difficult to move into a totally unfamiliar environment in which one knows neither language, places, people, nor characteristic patterns of expectation. For an immigrant from a peasant society coming to an industrial one, the change is considerable Peasants are used to a strongly kinship type of society with emphasis upon the family not the individual, on the clan, the village group not the individual. Thus we find these groups recreating and adapting their old institutions. It is a transition to a new culture, and it provides some stability, some comfort and psychic relaxation from the pressures that the immigrant finds in a new type of job. It also helps him learn the new ways from others who have gone through this process. He can maintain a sense of acceptance, self-esteem on grounds other than those on which the larger society may reject him.

If his housing looks old and run down compared to other sections of the area, it, like income, is more frequently a result rather than a cause of other attributes of social-class position.

Thus, we may be sure that the people will suffer psychologically if the community is destroyed.

What of the economic changes. Charles Hartman's study of 30 major urban renewal projects across the country found, that in all of them, people who relocated paid more for housing, either in rent or mortgages than they were paying previously. Some doubled their housing costs. In none were they paying the same or less. In some cases they got better housing for higher prices, in some cases the same kind of housing was found for higher prices, but "none could find cheaper or equivalent prices at the same level housing" (1964:266-286). More important, families are generally forced to pay higher rents for their new housing, often amounting to an unreasonable share of their income. In the Boston Westend, the median rent/income ratio for the relocated families went from 13.5% to 18.6%. In Chicago it went from 16.5% to 26.3% (ibid: 272, 273). Breaking this latter study down by income level, he discusses the degree to which *poorer families suffer most from these increases:*

> ". . . among those earning less than $3,000 per year (35% of all households) median rent/income ratio rose from 35.3 percent before relocation to 45.9 percent after relocation; among those in the $3000-$3999 bracket, the median ratio increased from 18.3 percent to 25.4 percent; and among those earning over $5000, the median ratio increased from 9.1 percent to 17.4 percent" (ibid:273).

Wolf and Lebeaux found in their study of six major relocation areas in Detroit that:

> "Relocated people are often found in better housing simply because most remaining housing is not likely to be as substandard as that demolished but which is more costly and leaves them less to spend on education, medical care, clothes and new televisions" (1966)

It was established by the court that the City had already destroyed a free market in the area and had made insufficient offers for the homes they purchased. The area is the largest and lowest renting area in Dearborn with a medium gross rent of $81.00 (Census 1970:100, H-25, H-26). It would be very difficult for either the home owners whose homes had been purchased by the City or the renters to relocate within the City under the conditions of the past few years.

Thus this community is being asked to sacrifice socially, psychologically and economically while Ford Motor Co. builds housing for upper income persons and the City builds homes for senior citizens in Florida.

Conclusion

In this essay, we have seen another example of the abuses of "urban renewal". In this case it has attempted to destroy a primary community of low and middle income laborers. The community has been characterized by overlapping social, economic and psychological relations. The people identify strongly with the community and most do not want to leave it or see its destruction, they would like to see it renewed. The pressures of the city are forcing divisions as well as a new community reorganization. The groups that will benefit from the community's destruction are big business and the more affluent Dearborn residents. It is obviously a case of class dominance and exploitation and it simultaneously appears to have the overtones of ethnic discrimination. In many ways it is analogous to the methods of dominance and exploitation of a colonized or imperialized region by outside powers, and can be likened to the treatment of the Black ghettos in the U.S. The Federal court has ruled that the methods of destruction by the City were illegal, however there are legal methods which involve more financing, citizen participation and time. The future remains uncertain for the community.

NOTES

[1]The author wishes to thank Mr. Alen Amen, President of the Southeast Dearborn Community Council, for his assistance and interest in this study.

[2]The Air Pollution Control Division of the Wayne County Health Department found that in 1971, the air in this area had "on the average twice as many suspended particulates-dust, flyash coke, iron oxides (to name a few) as the federal standards permit for health. On some days, it has more than three times the maximum." (Jo Thomas 1972). "The Ford Rouge Plant put 131.144 tons of Sulfur Dioxide and 2,000 tons of particulates in the air in 1971. This combination is the highest of any industry in the Detroit area." (Detroit Free Press 1972) The Health Department filed a suit against Ford and in Aug. 1973 a Consent Judgement was reached which required Ford to take 26 corrective actions to clean up the contamination. (Wayne County Health Dept. 1973) This action will certainly make the area a more desirable residential one.

[3]Another lower and middle income Middle Eastern community is composed of the recent migrants of the Chaldean community of Detroit and Highland Park. These are mainly small retail merchants.

[4]For example in 1968 Syria's GNP was $998.9 million, and its budget was $260.5 million. (The Middle East and North Africa:691). Lebanon, Yeman and Jordan have lower financial assets than Syria (Ibid.; 442, 846, 394). In the same year, Ford's sales were $14 billion, its operating income was $1 billion 278 million, and it's net income was $626 million. (Ford Motor Co. 1968:35). In 1972 their sales rose to $20 billion (Ibid 1972).

[5]Detroit's comparable median income is $7,944. Those households living below the poverty level for all of Detroit are 16.4%, but some areas reach as high as 45% (Census 1970; 227). The South End Census tract is number 839.

[6]See D. Epstein (1972) for an excellent discussion of the relationship of squatter settlements to urban areas in Brazil.

[7]The 1970 census lists 1695 occupied housing units, (p. 101) so this is approximately a 10% sample of household heads, either male or female.

[8]Heavier sample was done South of Dix Road. and in blocks with multiple dwelling units.

[9]Some of the villages of origin are Bint Ijbail, Tibnine, Aitzut etc.

[10]The income range for the South End is: (Census: 1970, p. 251)

Under $1,000	44 Households
$1,000 —$ 4,999	185 Households
$5,000 —$ 9,999	369 Households
$10,000—$14,999	364 Households
$15,000—$24,999	175 Households
$25,000—$49,000	20 Households
$50,000+	0 Households

[11]These regions include principally the cities of Hamtramck, Ypsilanti and Livonia.

[12]There are other smaller Muslim groups in Detroit. There is an Albanian mosque in East Detroit. This is attended primarily by non-Arab Sunni Muslims such as Albanians, Turks, Pakistani etc. There is also an Albanian Shia religious order called the Bektashi in Taylor Michigan a surburb of Detroit.

[13]Other ethnic groups in the South End support their own nationality clubs, such as the Italian-American Club, the Romanian Club and the Roman Hall. For some male members of these other ethnic groups, bars serve as local meeting places.

[14]SEDCC was joined in the case by another community organization from a smaller area called the Eugene-Porath area, which was also scheduled for industrial use. That area contains about 150 homes and is predominantely Polish in ethnic composition.

[15]Members of the AAUG who were active include Mr. Amen, President of the SEDCC Abdeen Jabara a lawyer who acted as Council for the Plaintiffs in the court case and two members who served as expert wittnesses for the Plaintiffs, Professor Zahour Yusuf and the author. A newly formed group, ACCESS (Arab Community Center For Economic and Social Services) has been helping the community in a number of ways. It is headed by a member of the AAUG, George Khoury.

BIBLIOGRAPHY AND REFERENCES

Abu-Lughod, Janet

    1961   "Migrant Adjustment and City Life: The Egyptian Case," *American Journal of Sociology,* Vol. 47, No. 1, pp. 22-32.

Amen et. al. v City of Dearborn et. al.

    1973a   Plaintiffs Trail Brief. (____F. Supp.____), Civil No. 37242 E.D. Michigan.

1973b   Opinion of the Court, August 14, 1973. (____F. Supp. ____),
         Civil No. 37242 E.D. Michigan.

Aswad, Barbara C.
1971   *Property Control and Social Strategies: Settlers on a Middle
         Eastern Plain.* Anthropological Papers No. 44, Museum of
         Anthropology, University of Michigan, Ann Arbor.

1973   *Results of Study on Southeast Dearborn.* First Series Revised.
         (Mimeograph).

1974   "Visiting Patterns among Elite Women in a Small Turkish
         City," *Anthropological Quarterly.* Winter issue (in press).

Breton, Raymond
1964   "Institutional Completeness of Ethnic Communities and the
         Personal Relations of Immigrants," *The American Journal of
         Sociology.* Vol. 7, No. 2, pp 193-205.

Breton, Raymond and M. Pinard
1960   "Group Formations Among Immigrants: Criteria and
         Progress," *Canadian Journal of Economics and Political
         Science,* Vol. 26 No. 3, pp 465-477.

Dearborn, City of
1970   Dearborn Michigan. Research and Information. City of
         Dearborn, Michigan.

Dearborn Police Department
1970   *Annual Report,* Dearborn, Michigan.

Detroit Free Press
1972   "Air Contaminants and Firms Listed:" July 9; p. 2. Detroit.

Elkholy, Abdo
1966   *The Arab Moslems in the United States: Religion and
         Assimilation.* New Haven College and University Press.

Epstein, David
1972   "The Genesis and Function of Squatter Settlements in Bra-
         silia," in *Anthropology in Urban Areas,* ed. by Thomas Weaver
         and Douglas White, The Society for Applied Anthropology,
         pp. 51-58.

Fitzpatrick, J.
1966   "The Importance of "Community" in the Process of Immi-

grant Assimilation," *The International Migration Review*. Vol. 1, No. 1 pp. 5-16.

Ford Motor Co.
  1968   *Annual Report*. 1968. Dearborn Michigan.

  1972   *Annual Report*. 1972. Dearborn Michigan.

Fried, Marc
  1963   "Grieving for a Lost Home," in Leonard J. Duhl, ed. *The Urban Condition*. New York: Basic Books.

Fried, Marc and Joan Levin
  1968   "Some Social Functions of the Urban Slum," in *Urban Planning and Social Policy*, ed. by Bernard J. Frieden and Robert Morris. New York: Basic Books.

Frieden, Bernard J. and Robert Morris
  1968   *Urban Planning and Social Policy*. New York: Basic Books.

Gans, Herbert
  1962   *The Urban Villagers*. New York: The Free Press.

Gonzales, Nancy
  1961   "Family Organization and Five Types of Migratory Labor," *American Anthropologist*, Vol. 63, pp. 1264-

Hagopian, Elaine and Ann Paden (eds.)
  1969   *The Arab-Americans*. Wilmette, Ill: Medina University Press International.

Hartman, Chester
  1963   "Social Values and Housing Orientations," *Journal of Social Issues*, XIX; 113-131.

  1964   "The Housing of Relocated Families," *Journal of the American Institute of Planners:* XXX; 266-286.

Kolm, Richard
  1971   "Ethnicity in Society and Community," in *Ethnic Groups in the City,* ed. by Otto Feinstein, Lexington, Mass.: Heath Lexington Books.

Leeds, A., and E. Leeds
  1967   "Brazil and the Myth of Urban Reality; Urban Experience, Work and Values in "Squatments" of Rio de Janeire and

Lima." Paper presented at the Conference on *Work and Urbanization in Modernizing Societies*, St. Thomas, Virgin Islands.

Rainwater, Lee
1968   "Fear and the House-as-Haven," in *Urban Planning and Social Policy*, ed. by Bernard Frieden and Robert Morris. New York: Basic Books.

Tabb, William K.
1970   *The Political Economy of the Black Ghetto*. New York: W.W. Norton.

The Middle East and North Africa 1969-70.
1969   Europa Publications Limited. London

Thomas, Jo
1972   "Our Air Can Sicken You, even Far from Factories." Detroit Free Press, July 9, pp. 1 and 2. Detroit.

U.S. Bureau of the Census
1970   Census of Population and Housing: 1970. Census Tracts. Final Report PHC (1)-58, Detroit Michigan. S.M.S.A.

1960   Census of Population and Housing, 1960. Census Tracts. Final Report PHC (1)-40. Detroit Michigan. S.M.S.A.

Wasfi, A.A.
1964   *Dearborn Arab-Moslem Community: A Study of Acculturation*. Unpublished Ph.D. Dissertation, East Lansing: Michigan State University.

Wayne County Health Dept., Air Pollution Control Division
1973   Highlights of Air Pollution Control Program, Court Approved Consent Judgement, Ford Motor Co. Rouge Complex. Detroit.

Wigle, Lauri
1972   "A Michigan Arab Muslim Community." (A chapter in this volume.)

Wolf, E. and C. Lebeaux
1969   *Change and Renewal in an Urban Community: Five Case Studies of Detroit*. New York: Praeger.

1966   "On the Destruction of Poor Neighborhoods by Urban Renewal." Paper read at the American Sociological Assoc. Sept. Miami, Fl.

The Migration of a Minority

CHARLES L. SWAN AND LEILA B. SABA[1]

Of the two really pivotal revolutions in human culture, the Neolithic and the Industrial, the first originated among the people of Palestine and their near neighbors, and the second, though it originated elsewhere, is currently engulfing the people of that area in some difficult adjustments. The contemporary Palestinians have two choices, which, of course, their ancient ancestors were not permitted: they may remain in Palestine and cold-hammer new forms of culture on the anvils of indigenous resources, or they may slip away quietly, as the subjects of this essay have, to join the industrial societies where the resources are currently more abundant.

When the choice is made, it is not at the prompting of any purely spontaneous impulse; cultural priorities of historic origin provide the decisive criteria. Out of the Neolithic configurations of the Palestinean milieu, a mosaic of cultural pluralisms emerged through the centuries, and we must take note of these pluralisms if we are to understand why certain groups made their particular choices to remain or to migrate. We must also note that the energies of the Industrial Age promise to fuse the ancient mosaic into an aggregate of uncertain design, and not all of the ancient minorities in the area are prepared to participate in such a fusion in the same fashion.

The majority of the members of the Christian Arab community of

Ramallah has migrated to the United States in the past half century. It is the purpose of this essay to develop the hypothesis that this migration had at least two salient motivations. Emigration from Palestine was prompted by a foreboding that the ethnic identity of Christian Ramallah may be doomed in the changing Middle East. At the same time immigration into the United States became attractive because here the modernizing modes of the Industrial Revolution seem to have evolved a temper which permits a tolerance of cultural pluralism, a tolerance which promises hopes for the continued integrity of the community and its cultural heritage. It is not the purpose of this paper to demonstrate that the people of Ramallah have been correct in their foreboding or expectations. Nor is it suggested that the motives here attributed to the Christian Arabs have at any time been given conscious or explicit formulation by the migrants. It is simply proposed to present the data which have suggested the hypothesis to the authors of this essay.

In the first place, it is suggested that events in the history of the Christian Arabs of Ramallah have generated in the members of the community what Arnold Rose has well termed, "Group identity" (1963:648). Their experience as members of a Christian minority among Arab Moslems has produced in the people of Ramallah a "sense of unity" which "involves not only a recognition that one is a member of a . . . religious group because of one's ancestry, nor only a recognition that the majority group defines one as belonging to the religious group. It involves a positive desire to identify oneself as a member of the group, and a feeling of satisfaction when one does so identify oneself" (Ibid.:685). It is further suggested that migration to the United States may well be motivated by what Merton has referred to as "anxiety accompanying the degrouping process" (1957:275), a process involved in the modernization of Palestine.

The Christian Arabs of Ramallah first appear in history in the early 1500s, (History of El Haddadeen 1951). When a group calling themselves *El Haddadeen* are found settled in the Shobak Kerak region of the Jordanian plateau east of the Dead Sea. It is from members of this group that the lineages of Ramallah's present community count their inheritance.

Traditions of *El Haddadeen* regarding an earlier history convey the impression that the group regards its marginal relationship with Arab society as one of very early origin. On philological grounds the forefathers are thought by some to have been Blacksmiths and by others "men of the border" (Ibid.): iron-workers, in Arabian lands as elsewhere, frequently hold a marginal status (Doughty 1946:1,-324-327) and groups which live on the northern borders of the desert tend to emphasize agriculture to a degree which marks them as separate from their bedouin neighbors.

Probably *El Haddadeen* were among the peoples consolidated under the Christian Ghassanids of Roman times.[2] It is thought (Kasees 1970:140) that in this period *El Haddadeen* were converted to Christianity, a circumstance which certainly solidified their minority status.

Centuries under the Ottomans did not modify this marginality. The "millet system" which the Istanbul regime inherited from earlier times gave to each minority group a great deal of internal independence and religious freedom. It was under this regime that *El Haddadeen* migrated from the Kerak region westward across the Jordan to the Ramallah site with which they have since become identified.

The story of the migration as traditionally preserved reveals something of the values which marked and preserved the group's ethnic identity. The migration became necessary when a strong herding tribe, *El Kayasmeh,* intruded upon the meadow lands controlled by *El Haddadeen.* Because the herders were powerful, resistance was futile, and for a number of years the agricultural Christians maintained peaceful relations with the pastoral Muslims, but this peace was broken when *El Kayasmeh* proposed a marriage between their chieftain's son and the daughter of Sabra El Haddad, the leader of the Christian group. *El Haddadeen* could tolerate economic symbiosis and political alliance with the Muslim group, but violation of religious endogamy, with its implication of ethnic assimilation, was wholly unacceptable. They preferred to leave their lands and move westward. The words of Sabra El Haddad marking their decision to move have become a motto of the people: "Fi el mal wala fi el rijah," signifying that a disgrace of property is easier to bear than disgrace of honor and religion (History of El Haddadeen 1951).

The new community at Ramallah retained full control of its own institutions and maintained its group identity. The town which grew up among the fields and orchards of *El Haddadeen* remained ethnically segregated, and until recently practically all the inhabitants of the town traced their descent to Sabra El Haddad and his two wives. It is therefore appropriate to speak of the group as "The People of Ramallah".

Contact with the outside world was limited, but because Ramallah was located only ten miles from the shrine city of Jerusalem it was inevitable than its Christian people should mingle occasionally in the stream of pilgrims from the Western world. This led to the opening of the doors of the community towards the West.

In 1858, Hanna Ibrahim Al-Saah joined a band of Greek Pilgrims (History of El Haddadeen 1951) on their return to Europe, taking with him a supply of sacred souvenirs for sale in the Churches of Istanbul and other cities. In this he initiated a movement which may be said to have reached its climax in the modern migration of the great majority of the people of Ramallah to America.

Interest in the West was given a powerful stimulus by the establishment in 1889 of two schools, one for girls and one for boys, by the English Quakers (Society of Friends). These institutions personalities trained in the West into the interaction patterns of the Ramallah community, and a number of young men and women were enculturated into the linguistic traditions and work-ways of the West. This meant that by the time the Ottoman rule was ended and the British mandate established in 1918, a generation of Ramallah youths had been prepared for employment in the mandatory bureaucracy which the British soon developed.

As Jerusalem grew in importance as a commercial and administrative center after 1918, the people of Ramallah acquired good positions in the city, and Ramallah became a pleasant residential suburb. It was inevitable that the experiences of this period should accentuate Western influences in the community. This does not mean that the people developed psychological or social identification with their British employers. The British historically have earned a reputation for permitting only the minimal official relationships with populations under their administration, and it can be said that the relationship of the people of Ramallah with the British differed little from the sub-social, symbiotic relationship which they had maintained with their Muslim neighbors for centuries.

With the rise of political tensions in Palestine between indigenous Arabs, the growing number of Jewish immigrants, and the bureaucratic British mandate authorities, the people of Ramallah found themselves in an anomalous position. They appreciated the legal protections and economic opportunities of the mandate period, but they felt, with others, the necessity for genuine participation in political decisions. At the same time they wished to preserve their ethnic distinctiveness from their Muslim neighbors and they found no common bonds with the Jewish immigrants.

With the end of the mandate and the partition of Palestine in 1948, they met new difficulties. Since they had developed no emotional ties with the British, they were prepared to serve any new employer in a progessive Jerusalem. But the division of Jerusalem and the removal of their governmental headquarters to Amman, far to the East, dislocated all the patterns of employment which they had developed during the mandate. Most disturbing also was the influx of Muslim Arab refugees into their comfortable, long-segregated suburb from the territories occupied by Israel. The seemingly massive incursion of these unfortunate members of the Muslim majority posed a threat to their ethnic identity, and emigration became attractive. The choice was not difficult to make to leave Palestine and move westward to join the Industrial Revolution in the Christian West where the modes of change seemed to permit greater freedom for the preservation of their heritage.

The evidence seems, then, to support the first hypothesis of this paper, that the movement of the people of Ramallah to the United States represents a continuation of their cultural history. They have been impelled by an unbroken tradition of marginality in their relations with their Muslim Arab neighbors. They have left their ethnic home because they feared they could not preserve ethnic identity in the emergent Middle Eastern setting.[3] In part they had been prepared for life in Western society with less tension and dislocation than they expected to face in their homeland.

The second hypothesis of this paper deals with the attraction of the American milieu. It may be asked, "Have the people of Ramallah found that the American setting is indeed more congenial, or at least more tolerant of pluralism, than the Palestinian milieu seemingly promised to be?"

To answer this question, we shall first examine the community formed in America by the people of Ramallah as a social entity. We shall assess as nearly as possible the likelihood that this community will persist in the American setting. Then we shall examine certain distinctive cultural and social structures in the life of the community and note whether each of the structures is likely to be maintained by the descendants of the immigrants.

It is appropriate first to look at the community life of the people of Ramallah as they have established themselves in America, to trace where possible the web of interactions within the group, and to assess the durability of the community in the new setting. In Palestine the people of Ramallah lived in a single town and were closely identified with this "ethnic home". This is not their experience in the United States.

There is some degree of concentration. Circumstances have led to the development of three major centers in which the majority of immigrants have settled: Detroit, Michigan; Washington, D.C.; and Jacksonville, Florida. In each of these centers some two thousand members of the Ramallah community have settled. However, these three major centers are large metropolitan communities, and within their extended boundaries the people of Ramallah have formed no concentrated residential section. Indeed, during the years of their migration they never, even temporarily, developed a "Ramallah quarter" or "port of entry". The Ramallah families have moved directly to homes scattered widely through the three metropolitan centers.[4]

It may now be asked if this residential dispersion offers any basis for prediction regarding the future cohesiveness of the Ramallah community or regarding its continued ethnic integrity.

It is always hazardous to make predictions concerning the continuity of immigrant cultures in the American setting. Many groups have sought to preserve their identity by migrating to the "wide open spaces" and reputedly generous pluralisms of America, and their experiences in the new world have been highly diverse. Nevertheless it is possible to abstract a generalized pattern from the complex of history and suggest some basic principles for assessing the durability of migrant cultures.

First, we find that some groups have developed mechanisms which diminish acculturative and assimilative contacts to an absolute minimum by organizing what may be called "ethnic enc-laves". These groups have encapsulated themselves in self-sufficient neighborhoods where their social and economic activities have been almost completely independent of majority interference. The prototype of the "ethnic enclave" is the well-known community formed by the Old Order Amish Mennonite Church in Pennsylvania. (Hostetler, 1968:131f.)

Few immigrant groups have developed comparable enclaves. Certainly the people of Ramallah have not done so. The differences between the Ramallah migration and the migration of the persecuted Mennonite Germans are many. The Amish people came to America early in the eighteenth century out of an agricultural economy into a country where land was plentiful for the taking. The Ramallah people arrived in the mid-twentieth century. When the Amish migrated, subsistence farming was the dominant occupation of the people of the country they left as it was for the people in the new world; their enclaves are essentially continuations into the modern age of patterns which were general at the time of their founding as a Christian sect, patterns of technology and social interaction which became sanctioned by their religious ideology. The people of Ramallah were introduced to modern industrial and bureaucratic practice before leaving their ethnic home and have arrived at a time when these new skills meant survival and participation in the society of the new home. For the Amish the German language could be used freely in the new world because it was possible for them to conduct their subsistence farming without dependence upon English speaking neighbors; the German language—as they spoke it—became a boundary-maintaining device, a mark of distinction for them, strengthening their isolation against acculturative influences. In their agricultural setting they have been able not only to preserve a spatial separation, but their entire "ordrung", governing their clothing, their patterns of family authority, their religious rites, their educational institutions, has been free to perpetuate itself in cultural isolation (Hosteller: 1968:59). So they have maintained their isolation and cultivated their ethnic identity for some three centuries. For the people of Ramallah the skills they brought with them meant successful assimilation in the economic and industrial structures of the new world, if not in the social structures. For them an "ethnic enclave" was not only un-thinkable; it was not feasible.

Consequently we cannot expect the people of Ramallah to repli-cate the exclusiveness of the Amish people; we cannot expect them to hold to their traditional patterns over many generations in isolation.

A second type of adjustment to the American setting may be called the "ethnic village". Herbert Gans's classic study of Italian "urban villagers" in Boston suggests this title (1962). In these concentrations, some of them agricultural but most of them in-dustrial, residential proximity has provided certain survival services to the immigrants. These "villages" are neighborhoods in which the language of the ethnic home is spoken by most of the residents because most of the members of the group do not use the English language; indeed the immigrants seek residence in these "villages" because they must depend upon their compatriots for most of the necessities of life, social, religious, economic. The "ethnic village" is not economically independent and many economic necessities originate outside the "village"; most important, most opportunities for employment are found outside the "village". However, within the concentration numbers of institutions have been developed by which social needs thought to be essential are met, and the familiar culture of the ethnic home is preserved. Some non-English-speaking Muslim Arabs have established "ethnic villages" in the cities of America (Elkholy 1966 and Aswad this volume). But the Christian Arabs from Ramallah have not found it necessary to do so. They were already sufficiently familiar with the institutions, economic and social, of the Western world to achieve a comfortable adjustment without segregation in an "ethnic village".

The history of "ethnic villages" has been various. Agricultural neighborhoods, most of them centering upon Lutheran or Catholic churches, have maintained many of their ethnic characteristics to the fourth and fifth generations. Like all American agricultural communities the "ethnic villages" of rural America have lost members to growing urban centers of the country; the scarcity of agricultural land, the desire to maintain farm size, and the inviting prospects of city life have contributed to the steady drain of man-power from rural "ethnic villages". This drain has been accompanied by a reverse acculturative influence. In general it may be said that the rural "ethnic village" has been only slightly less vulnerable to assimilation than the urban "ethnic village". The urban "village" has suffered from individual mobility, as the agricultural "village" has. But its chief difficulty has been urban change. The process of invasion and succession, with the resulting change in the ethnic character of any given section of the city, has marked the history of the American city, and urban "ethnic villages" have been swept along in successive tides of migration. In more recent years, "urban renewal" and the drive to eliminate "obsolescent" housing has liquidated a number of urban "ethnic villages"; the West End "Village" of Gans's study was destroyed soon after the completion of his work by "urban renewal". So the fate of the "ethnic village", whether rural or urban, has varied, but in none of them has the traditional culture remained untouched.

A third form of ethnic adjustment in America has been what we call "the ethnic community". The term "community" is used without precision in the social sciences; it may be applied to any social entity from the rural "enclave" to the nation state as a whole. Lenski (1970:41) has helped to clarify usage by distinguishing between "geographical communities" and "cultural communities". The former are "united primarily by ties of spatial proximity", the latter by "ties of a common cultural tradition". "Ethnic communities" are to be thought of as united by the ties of the specific ethnic heritage of an immigrant group. Such communities may share any geographical area with other ethnic communities, but they must develop patterns of communication if they are to maintain their identity. Ethnic communities involve such elemental networks as those based on kinship and personal friendship. They usually develop voluntary associations of many sorts, including churches and ethnic societies, which provide means for continuous contacts between the members of the community. Common memories, a common language, common values and an assortment of "cultural" interests (in literature, the arts, food and festivals) provide the content of their interaction. In many cases the economic and political fate of the "old country" provides a continuing center of concern. The existence of an ethnic press, or at least a periodical, marks a living ethnic community. Religious schools frequently serve not only to socialize the American-born generations to the religious culture but also to teach the language, history and cultural values of the ethnic traditions. Some "ethnic communities" in America have developed a rich complex of institutional patterns around the ethnic interest, patterns which persist despite wide dispersal of residence.

The "ethnic community" is the pattern of adjustment achieved by the people of Ramallah in their three centers in the United States. The center of interaction in each case has not been a "ethnic church", for the community is religiously divided, but in the "Ramallah association" which has its local organization as well as a national organization. The "Haithihe Ramallah" is a periodical published by the Detroit organization and distributed nationally, which serves as a means of general communication.

The most frequent and effective means of interaction are the occasions when a wedding is celebrated between members of the community; funerals have been less frequent. Two grocery stores owned by Ramallah families, though not located centrally in the metropolitan area, are places for face-to-face meetings by some members of the community. The "life blood" of the community, however, flows through personal conversations on the telephone, through visits between the families of kinfolk and friends, facilitated by the American automobile, and through the general interaction spurred by a desire to keep in touch with "people from back home". In most of these interactions, the Arabic language is the medium of communication for the older members of the community. For young members, particularly for the men, the English of the business world is often the most satisfactory means for reaching understandings. The durability of such a community depends upon the continuity of kinship ties and friendships, rather than upon institutionalized systems of cooperation. Of the tenacity of kinship and friendship a more detailed study is offered below.

It should be pointed out that an "ethnic community" depends upon the development in successive generations of a high quality of leadership, for it will be necessary in each generation (if not more often) to continuously re-interpret the ethnic heritage in terms which make it relevant to the members who live in the changing environment of American society without any mechanisms isolating them from the change.

Ethnic consciousness may take a fourth form in the American set-ting, a form we may call the "Ethnic public". We use the term "public" to refer, as Horton and Hunt put it, to "a scattered number of people who share an interest in a particular topic" (Horton and Hunt 1972:400). When an immigrant group becomes highly assimilated, its members may retain "an interest" in the af-fairs of the ethnic home or in aspects of the ethnic culture, an interest expressed in their support of publications of the mass media in one way or another. This sort of "interest" may endure through several generations because of a feeling of identity with "family history" or "family name", or because of an emotionally tinged in-tellectual interest.

The four forms of ethnic adjustment described as the "ethnic en-clave", the "ethnic village", the "ethnic community" and the "ethnic public" may serve as something more than a typology. They may suggest a series of successive stages in the process of ass-milation and acculturation. There are difficulties in using the ty-pology as a description of process. Most groups never adjust in the pattern of the "ethnic enclave"; they usually begin as "ethnic villages" or, as in the case of the people of Ramallah, as "ethnic communities". Instances of continuing "ethnic publics" are hard to find. Furthermore, the typology does not help us measure the rate of change, the pace at which a group may be expected to pass from one type to the next. Any measurement of such change would have to be given in generations, but groups differ greatly in the number of generations spent at any one "stage". Nevertheless the typology may have use in suggesting what the next form of adjustment is likely to be after the institutions of one form cease to be operative. And it may be said that no group can be expected to function permanently at any one stage without conscious effort and considerable organizational skill. Even the Old Order Amish Men-nonites have lost members from their "enclaves": the numerous "splinters" in the Mennonite movement manifest the influence of acculturation in the group.

In summary, then, the people of Ramallah clearly constitute in their three major centers "ethnic communities". They have not at any time developed "ethnic enclaves" or "ethnic villages". They have not become a mere "ethnic public". To assess the durability of their community structures further, it is necessary to examine a number of characteristics important to their community life. Following the work of Sengstock in her study of the Iraqi Chaldean community in Detroit, (1967), a study which demonstrated the usefulness of distinguishing between acculturation on the one hand and social assimilation on the other, the variables examined here are classified as (1) the cultural factors and (2) the social factors. Taking a cue from Gordon, (1964:716) the cultural factors are divided between (a) cultural norms and values and (b) group identity, while the social factors include (a) associational patterns and (b) intermarriage.

The present study is confined to the community of the people of Ramallah living in Detroit. A random sample of sixty-six heads of families, all males, were interviewed. All but one of these respondents were born in Ramallah, and the one exception, though born in the United States returned to Ramallah in very early life and lived there until as an adult he migrated permanently and settled in Detroit.

(1) Cultural Factors
(a) Cultural Norms and Values:
(i) A fundamental factor in cultural persistence has been the language of the ethnic group. Information received from the respondents indicated that the people of Ramallah were generally bi-lingual even before migrating to America. Of respondents to the interview, twenty-nine percent confessed to some inadequacy in their use of the English language, but 71% declared that they spoke English "fairly well" or "very fluently" upon their arrival in the United States. They regard Arabic as their mother tongue. Indeed the Arabic of the Ramallah people is regarded, by themselves at least, as in the classic form of bedouin usage in Arabia. But efforts to preserve the use of the language to American-born generations is confined to the families where children are spoken to in Arabic. It is reported that grade school children are inclined to respond in English when their parents address them in Arabic, and it is sometimes difficult to be consistent in requiring them to use Arabic. It would appear that in a large number of the Ramallah homes parents find English congenial for most purposes and Arabic is used irregularly.

It is difficult to believe that the upward-mobile, middle class

family can be expected to carry full responsibility for the preservation of the linguistic heritage; certainly continued use of the
Arabic language would seem to require extra-familial institutions,
especially if it is to retain its full, mature literary quality. It is un-
likely that a language will persist among people who study English
as the language of mature, adult thought and retain the mother
tongue only as a domestic option applied largely to children's
concerns. Formal patterns for the continued study of the Arabic
language seem to be a matter which should concern the leadership
of the community if it desires the preservation of the ethnic
identity.

(ii) Norms governing authority in the family are important
cultural factors in any group. To study the norms of the Detroit
families, a number of questions were asked of the sample of male
heads of households.

A forthright statement of belief in patriarchal authority was
presented to respondents: "A father's word should be final in a
home; without obedience to the father a family cannot enjoy peace
and contentment." Over one-third of the respondents (37.5%) gave
the statement their unqualified assent. Only 15.2% felt it was
"untrue". But the largest group, 45.5% felt the statement should be
regarded as "doubtful".

An effort was made to discover if there is any tendency to change
in their acceptance of this norm of patriarchal authority as a result
of American acculturative influences. The sample was divided into
three groups, the older group, a middle-aged group, and a younger
group, each with the same number of respondents. Comparisons
between the older group and the younger group, between whom
the largest differences might be expected, were made with tests of
statistical significance. It was found that in their responses to this
forthright statement on patriarchal control, the youngest group did
not differ from the oldest group, and that therefore no great change
seems to be taking place on the matter in the American setting.

To discover what the actual patterns are in the homes of the
people of Ramallah on this matter of paternal authority was, of
course, beyond the scope of this study. But respondents were asked
to express an opinion on what proportion of families in the Ramallah community actually maintain the traditional paternal au-

thority in practice. They were asked to indicate their opinion on conditions both in Ramallah, the ethnic home, and in the Detroit community. Of the respondents, 25.8% said that *all* families in Ramallah are patriarchal in actual practice, but only 9.1% ventured the opinion that *all* families in Detroit practice patriarchal authority; 50% of respondents felt that of the families in Ramallah 75% are patriarchal in practice, while only 41.8% estimated that of Detroit families 75% practice patriarchal authority. Thus, in the opinion of over three-quarters of the heads of household in Detroit, of Palestinian Ramallah families 75% practice patriarchal authority, while less than one half of the respondents felt that 75% of Detroit families are patriarchal in practice. The data suggest, therefore, that Detroit men feel that fathers hold authority much more generally in the homes of people back in Ramallah than they do in the homes of the Detroit migrants.

When the youngest group of respondents was compared with the oldest, a difference was discovered. The younger men felt that patriarchal authority was practiced less frequently in Ramallah than did the older men. They also felt that Detroit families were less patriarchal than the older men did. In other words, the younger group does not feel the same assurance that patriarchal authority continues to govern family life which the older men expressed.

In traditional Arab families, the authority of parents is perhaps most clearly demonstrated in their selection of brides for their sons. Six statements of opinion regarding parental control in bride selection (or groom selection) were presented to the respondents. Table 1 indicates their responses:

TABLE 1
Attitudes towards Parental Authority
in the Selection of Marriage Partners

| | | Responses | |
Statements	True %	Doubtful %	Untrue %
1. Sons should let parents select their brides.	7.6	12.1	80.3
2. Sons may select their brides but should not go against the judgment of their parents.	36.4	33.3	30.3
3. Sons should select their own brides and parents should not interfere.	40.9	30.3	28.8
4. Daughters should let their parents select their husbands.	10.6	21.2	68.2
5. Daughters should select their husbands but should not go against the advice of their parents.	66.7	21.2	12.1
6. Daughters should select their own husbands and parents should not interfere.	30.3	30.3	37.9°

° No answer, 1.5%

It will be seen that only a small percentage of respondents take the forthrightly traditional pattern expressed in statements 1 and 4. One third of the respondents favor "giving the parents a veto power" over the selection of brides by sons, but two-thirds would allow "veto power" for parents of girls. Of respondents 40.9% favor a "hands off" policy in male mate selection; only 30.3% would give females the same complete freedom from parental control.

It is not surprising that there is a clear statistical difference between the youngest group and the oldest group of respondents on this matter of mate selection and parental controls. It is among the youngest group that we find support for complete freedom from parental interference. Change in the direction of diminished parental participation in mate selection tends to be a world-wide phenomenon, and the difference between the older and younger men cannot be attributed solely to the American milieu. It need not be regarded, therefore, as an indication of loss of ethnic identity; it simply means that parental control of mate selection is less and less an important factor in distinguishing the life of the Arab community from that of other communities, whether Western or Asian.

Arab culture is reported to regard cousin marriage—particularly parallel cousin marriage, whether patrilateral or matrilateral—as a preferential pattern. It is generally assumed that this tradition serves both to limit the freedom of choice of young people and to preserve the authority of the family in mate selection. In Western society cousin marriage has come to be frowned on for a variety of reasons, not all of them biological. It may be assumed therefore that disapproval of parallel cousin marriage indicates acculturation with the Western norms superceding the Arab norms. The responses showed that over a third of the respondents accepted the parallel cousin marriage as "very good" or "fair", but two-thirds of them rated it as "bad" or "very bad". Differences between the youngest group and the oldest group of respondents on the matter of cousin marriage was not statistically significant. This indicates that the tendency to discard the Arab preferences for parallel cousin marriage is not a matter related to rapid acculturation; changes in these norms may be said not to threaten ethnic identity.

Before proceeding to other cultural norms and values, it should be noted that Kassees, using the Bardis scale of "Familism", came to the conclusion that "the Ramallah people living in the United States were significantly more familistic than the Ramallah people living in Ramallah." (Kassees 1972) This finding would tend to suggest that the migration of the people of Ramallah to the United States was selective and weighted with conservative families. This would tend to support the thesis offered in the first part of this paper that the people of Ramallah have migrated to America in part to preserve their ethnic traditions, their ethnic identity. However, the data presented above would suggest that, either in the ethnic home or in the American setting, a good deal of change has taken place in norms governing patriarchal authority, parental control of mate selection and parallel cousin marriage. The differences between older men and younger men in their responses on these topics is not consistent, but in some matters, particularly in the matter of parental control of mate selection, the young tend to accept Western norms more completely than their seniors. The question then must be raised that if acculturation has not been successfully resisted, in these norms of family authority at least, will further acculturation be checked in the highly communicative setting of the Ramallah community in America?

(iii) The cultural values of Ramallah people in Detroit were explored by simply asking the open-ended question, "What are the important points which should be passed on to the young people about Ramallah and its history and traditions?"

Of the sample, fifteen heads of households ignored the question . . A sixteenth, a young man, replied, "I don't think there should be that much emphasis on Ramallah; it makes little difference where you come from." But the remaining fifty respondents mentioned a total of 108 items in their answers. The largest group of the answers (17.6% of them) simply referred to "our traditions" or "our culture", but the rest of the answers were more specific. References to the ethnic home, the town of Ramallah, were made by 34% of the respondents who answered this question. One respondent added, "Ramallah is our home; we shall return." Several mentioned the "famous climate" of Ramallah. Other subjects were mentioned less frequently. Of all answers, 14.8% urged emphasis on family unity, including the whole extended family; 12.1% of the answers referred to ethnic language, and the same number referred to the history of the people of Ramallah. Strengthening of group identity was called for in 11.1% of the responses; ethical training in a general way was suggested in 10.2% of the 108 answers. Specific culture traits were mentioned in only 5 of the 108 responses.

It would seem that the only aspect of their heritage which came to the minds of respondents in answering the open-ended question was the ethnic home, the geographical locus of their traditional culture. Awareness of specific elements in the heritage seems minimal. It would seem that if the community felt any stresses due to the threat of acculturation against any very precious culture traits, this stress would have found expression in answers to this question. The conclusion seems inevitable that either the American milieu does not threaten the heritage of the migrants or the migrants have no serious commitment to any specific cultural traits in their inheritance.

(iv) Of the "cultural values" revealed by the open-ended question, the religious heritage of the people of Ramallah was mentioned by only two individuals (4% of the responding heads of families). This suggests that there has been a fairly sharp break with the historic concerns of *El Haddadeen* who have persistently preserved their religious identity as Christians in the face of considerable Islamic pressure. The diminished significance of religion as a focus of ethnic identity is partly explained by the sectarian divisions which have taken place in the Ramallah community in Palestine. Until some time in the second half of the nineteenth century, *El Haddadeen* were united in a single congregation under the authority of the Syrian Orthodox Church, practicing the rites of Byzantium or "Roum" (the Eastern "Rome"). Records indicate that by 1700 the community had its own Syrian Orthodox basilica, and in that year the first local ordination of a priest was recorded. But at some time before 1895 the Roman Catholic congregation of Ramallah, using the "Lateen" rite, was established, and by 1944 two fifths of the Christian Arabs of Ramallah were following the "Lateen" discipline. In the twentieth century small gains were made by Protestant proselytizers. Thus before the migration to America, religion alone no longer served as an integrating center for the community. Even at Christmas and Easter, the members of the community were united, not by the church, but in simple formalities in the "city hall".

Consequently the community in Detroit has been without the "ethnic church" which has served so many other ethnic groups as a center for interaction and as a symbol of ethnic values.

(v) Ethnic endogamy, the data we collected would seem to show, continues to have considerable vitality. The respondents were presented with the statement, "It is better to marry Romallah people." Only 51.5% expressed undoubted approval of the statement, but a larger proportion, 63.6% expressed assent to the statement, "Marriage with other Arab Christians is almost always happy." These responses contrast strongly with the reactions to the statement, "Marriage with non-Christians is almost always happy;" to this statement only 7.6% responded that it was "true", 43.9% were doubtful about the statement and 45.5% declared it to be untrue. To the statement, "Marriage with Americans is almost always happy," 16.7% of respondents answered, "True"; 62.1% were "doubtful" and 21.2% were clearly opposed. These findings would suggest that the Arab Christian community, rather than the more narrowly defined community of the Ramallah people, constitutes the generally accepted endogamous grouping in the norms and values of the men of the community. Yet it must be acceded that endogamy still remains the bastion of ethnic identity in Detroit today as it served in the earlier history of *El Haddadeen*.

(b) Group Identity:

Cultural factors underlie the sense of group identity found among the people of Ramallah living in Detroit. To examine group identity several variables have been studied.

(i) Interest in the ethnic home is undoubtedly an important uniting and identifying interest. When asked if Ramallah is "a good place to live", 65.2% responded affirmatively, and one-third responded acknowledging that with its "good points" Ramallah has "some drawbacks". Only one responded that it has only "many drawbacks". Nearly half of the respondents (46.9%) reported that they had made at least one trip back to Palestine since migrating for settlement in the United States.

Ties with Ramallah continue; 83.3% claim to send large or small gifts to individuals, families or institutions in Ramallah, and business ties with Ramallah are regarded as "important" by 22.7% of the heads of households reporting, "relatively unimportant" by 18.2% (59.1 percent have no business ties with the home town).

Desire to return to Ramallah is conditional. Less than 10% want to return to their home under present conditions and immediately; 22.7% have more or less desire to return after retirement. However, if the Israeli occupation of the area is lifted, 59.1% would consider returning immediately and 93.9% would consider retiring in Ramallah (84.8% declare they would definitely retire in a Ramallah released from Israeli control).

(ii) Cultural factors connected with group identity underly the reasons for migration to America. These cannot be described with precision, but the motives for migration are suggestive of the effective values underlying important decision-making in the community. According to 63.6% of the respondents, financial reasons in themselves were not involved in the decision to migrate to

America; only 28.5% conceded that financial conditions were significant in leading to the decision to leave Palestine. Political
reasons and the Arab-Israeli conflict were decisive for only 19.7% of
the respondents (though these reasons play a very important part in
attitudes towards returning to Ramallah!) Employment opportunities seem to have been the most important consideration for most
of the migrants; 90.6% said "Yes," and 6.0% said "Perhaps" when
asked if migration was decided upon because of a desire to get employment or improved employment. Financial aid came to about
half the migrants from friends in America to make the migration
possible for them, and 69.7% reported that earlier migrants used
"persuasion" which helped them decide to leave for America. It
was evident that the most persuasive argument in favor of migration was the offering of employment in this country, but for
most of the migrants it was the fact that their fellow Ramallah
people were conveying the message which seems to have been the
most convincing factor in the situation. The over-all picture we get
from the data is that of a group of people with a common desire to
achieve superior levels of employment in a Western-type setting,
and aiding each other because of a sense of group identity.

(iii) This same group identity is evident from the responses to
questions designed to reveal the "group self image" of the people
of Ramallah in Detroit. Their responses indicate that these people
regard themselves as a predominantly prosperous and successful
group, with very few of their number failing to achieve good economic status. They regard themselves as a people with exceptionally high educational standards, especially when they are compared with other migrant groups newly arrived in America. Home
ownership is general: 18.2% own their homes outright, and 66.7%
are paying mortgages on homes.

(iv) Political opinions and interests in the group reveal a high
degree of group identity and a general similarity in their underlying interest in the political future of their Palestinian home-
land. A positive answer was given by 77.0% or more of the
respondents to the following statements:

"The American government is giving too much assistance to
Israel."

"The American government should recognize that the Arabs are more dependable friends than Israel."

"The American government should know that Arab states are more tolerant of religious minorities than Israel."

"The American people should send funds privately to Palestine."

"The Ramallah people in Detroit should work harder to persuade American politicians to give aid to the Arab cause."

"The Ramallah people in Detroit should themselves give more aid to the Arab Palestinians."

The "No" responses to these statements were negligible, but it may have some significance that 7.1% neglected to respond to these questions. The data would suggest, however, that the Ramallah people in Detroit have strong feelings of identity with their ethnic home, with those who have come with them from that home, and with the fate of that area in the political arena; they are, however, at the same time working sedulously, and remarkably successfully, to achieve standards of living, through employment and education, comparable to the levels of America's upper middle class, not merely in emulation of their American neighbors but, quite consciously, to keep up with the more successful members of their own community.

It is difficult on the basis of the above study of "cultural factors" to assert with any confidence that the people of Ramallah in Detroit have found in their community life an enduring foundation for their ethnic identity in a congenially pluralistic society. There is in the migrant generation which we have studied a high interest in the ethnic home, the Ramallah of their memories, at least. Some of the familistic traditions of their ethnic heritage are adhered to, but adherence is not at all universal or unquestioned. There seems to be no clear focus in the minds of the migrants as to what values in their heritage are central and most carefully to be preserved. Also, the Church and institutions for teaching the language to the younger generation, instruments for ethnic continuity which are usually regarded as essential, are not functional for the Ramallah community in Detroit. However, there is a very positive self image which has been developed in the community, and the fact that they generally regard themselves as a successful, well-educated and up-wardly mobile group enhances membership in the group.

(2) Social Factors

(a) Associational patterns are important to the study of community continuity among migrant groups in America. If associational pat-terns remain predominantly within the community continuity may be expected. If, however, members of the community interact increasingly with the neighbors of the American majority, assimilation may be expected to diminish community integrity ac-cordingly. There are several ways in which associational patterns have been studied.

(i) The first question which may be asked is, "Are there enough members of the community living in Detroit to permit the development of satisfactory in-group interaction patterns?" Of the heads of households questioned, 37.9% declared that over half of their kinfolk live in the Detroit area and 31.8% declared that between 25 and 50% of their kinfolk live in the community. No ef-fort was made to discover what was meant by "kinfolk" or "rela-tives". In the broadest sense all members of *El Haddadeen* are regarded as "kin", but in all probability the term for most respondents meant the "extended family" of mutual assistance. It is to be assumed that, with a large proportion of their rather extended kinship groups resident in the area, in-group interaction is possible on a satisfactory level.

(ii) To measure the intensity of ingroup interaction, respondents were asked what percentage of their "friendships" were with Ra-mallah people. Of the respondents 33.3% thought that all their friendships were within the Ramallah community; 24.2% felt that 75% or more of their friendships were in-group centered; 36.4% thought that a half or more of their friendships involved people out-side the Ramallah population. These percentages were somewhat lower than the friendships reported for the first year or two after migration, and it is evident that social assimilation, in the form of friendship contacts outside of the group, is increasing. But the data also show that a minority of Ramallah people found friends outside the community at the very beginning of their residence in America and that this group continues to lead the group in assimilative contacts.

(iii) The employment status of the Ramallah heads of household is revealing with regard to assimilative experience. Occupations which involve the greatest exposure to contacts with Americans of the majority are those of the professions, of management, of white collar occupations and of student status. Of the respondents 81.9% are in these occupations. Approximately 9.0% of the respondents are to be classified as in skilled or semi-skilled occupations and another 9.0% are unskilled; while these occupations are not without contacts with English speaking Americans, the work they perform is less "with people" or "with data" than is the work of "white collar" occupations. For the great majority of Ramallah men, it will be seen, the work place and the work responsibilities involve a maximum exposure to interaction with the majority population. Whether these work-place contacts will lead to a dissipation of in-group interaction for the people of Ramallah is yet to be seen.

(iv) Interest in the political life of the American scene may be used as an indicator of assimilative interaction. It is significant that only 12.1% find Detroit politics "very interesting", only 24.2% find that Michigan politics are "interesting", but National political activities are "very interesting" to 40.9%. It is possible that this greater interest in National politics is due to interest in the international aspects of national politics, particularly in aspects related to the Middle East. On the other hand, this may simply indicate that issues on the national scene at the time were more interesting than issues on the state or local scene.

v) Educational data does not help us measure the assimilative process with regard to social interaction outside the in-group. Of the respondents, 51.5% had all their education in Palestine, most of them completing much of their high school education. Only 10.0% had all their education in the United States. It would be presumed that the more education an individual has had in the United States, the more likely he would be to move freely in the circles of American friends. Actually Palestinian education, which has been predominently westernizing, does not offer any barriers to interaction with Americans. The fact that only 21.2% of the heads of household have failed to complete a high school education would indicate that the community generally is not hindered from interaction with the American neighbor because of educational deficiencies.

(b) Intermarriage between Ramallah people and their neighbors in the American setting is a matter of considerable interest in the study of the social factors and their role in community continuity. The data obtained in the study indicates, generally, that group endogamy continues to be the most common practice. Respondents were asked to recall the marriages of their brothers and sisters. They reported that 77.6% of their brothers and 87.5% of their sisters had married within ethnic lines. When the respondents were asked to estimate, on the basis of their impressions, how many young people of the Ramallah community have married within the ethnic group and how many had married "Americans", the consensus of opinion seems to suggest that 75% of more of all marriages, whether of the migrant generation or the first generation born in America, have been within the Ramallah membership. The population of *El Haddadeen* now resident in Detroit is probably sufficient to provide a fairly satisfactory selection of mates, so that with a little parental encouragement ethnic endogamy may continue for another generation or more.

In summary it may be said of the data on social factors of interaction that the people of Ramallah have an active in-group association, their kinship and friendship ties within the group being rich and numerous. Yet they are not without contacts with the majority society around them, their occupational experiences and their educational standards permitting free movement in American society. Group endogamy is still commonly maintained, but not all marriages are within the Ramallah membership. These findings seem to indicate that the people of Ramallah continue to maintain their group identity in significant ways, but they also show that the pluralistic society of the American setting, while tolerant of group identity, is also open to assimilative and free interaction which may lead to increasing disintegration of the community's internal patterns of interaction.

Finally, in regard to the second hypothesis of this paper, the hypothesis that the people of Ramallah have come to America attracted by a seemingly tolerant pluralism in which their group identity may be better preserved than in the Palestinian or the Israeli milieus, it may be said that up to the present the majority of the members of the group seem to have achieved a viable equilibrium between group identity and integration in the larger community of the majority. Acculturative and assimilative processes are indeed occuring; how long the centrifugal forces of in-group culture and society will restrain the centripetal tendencies of the situation it would at this juncture be impossible to predict.

NOTES

[1]Much of the material for this paper was collected by Miss Saba of Ramallah, Palestine, for her Master's thesis at Wayne State University in 1971. The organization of the paper and much of the interpretive point of view is the responsibility of the senior author. The advice of Dr. Mary Catherine Sengstock, and Dr. Barbara Aswad has been invaluable in giving final form to the paper.

[2]The Ramallah historians write of the Ghassanid age in eulogistic terms: "El Haddadeen were quite industrious people who mastered the art of irrigation and farming, which made their fields prosper with olive trees, grapes, figs, barley and corn; they also raised cattle." (Kassees 1970:40)

Here we may have a rudimentary "Golden Age" myth of the type frequently lending color and glamor to the self-image of minorities in the mosaic of Middle Eastern society. Such myths, with their claims of dynastic lineage and their memories of power in some specific period of history at some specific geographical locus, undoubtedly function to add durability to group identity. However, *El Haddadeen* have not elaborated their traditions of this "Golden Age", at least not to the extent found in some minorities. The Ramallah traditions cherish no charismatic culture hero, no extended literary heritage. The religious heritage deriving from the Ghassanid period is not entirely unique but is generically Eastern Orthodox. Even the geographical locus of their traditional "moment of glory" has lost its significance because the community became closely attached to the Palestinian site at Ramallah. Nevertheless, the Ghassanid age is not a forgotten part of their heritage, and confirms their identity as an historical minority.

The Ghassanids themselves were probably "outsiders" in Northern Arabia, for there are claims that they originated in the extreme south of Arabia in the age of the Sabaean civilization. (Thatcher and Hitti 1956: 188)

[3]Ramallah is located in the "West Bank" area of the Jordan River which has been under Israeli occupation since the war of 1967.

[4]In the Detroit region however, there has been some limited degree of regional clustering in the areas of Livonia and Garden City.

REFERENCES

Doughty, Charles M.
1946   *Travels in Arabia Deserta*. New York, Random House.

ElKholy, Abdo A.
1966   *The Arab Moslems in the United States*. New Haven, College
         and University Press.

Gans, Herbert J.
1962   *The Urban Villagers; Group and Class in the Life of Italian-
         Americans*. New York, The Free Press.

Gordon, Milton M.
1964   *Assimilation in American Life*. New York, Oxford University.

"History of El Haddadeen"
1951   Unpublished Manuscript; Ramallah, Jordan; (no pagination).

Horton, Paul and Hunt, Chester
1972   *Sociology*. Third Edition; New York, McGraw Hill Book Co.,

Hostetler, John A.
1968   *Amish Society*. Baltimore, Md., Johns Hopkins Press

Kassees, Assad S.
1970   *The People of Ramallah*. Unpublished Ph.D. Dissertation;
         Florida State University;

Kassees, Assad S.
1972   "Cross Cultural Comparative Familism of a Christian Arab
         People," *Journal of Marriage and the Family*, August 1972.

Lenski, Gerhard
1970   *Human Societies*. New York, McGraw Hill Book Company;

Merton, Robert K.
1957   *Social Theory and Social Structure*. Glencoe, Ills., The Free
         Press.

Rose, Arnold M.
1963   *Sociology: The Study of Human Relations*. Second Edition, New
         York, Alfred A. Knopf.

Sengstock, Mary C.
1967   *The Maintenance of Social Interaction Patterns in Ethnic
         Groups*. Unpublished Doctoral Dissertation; Washington
         University, St. Louis., Mo.

Thatcher, G. W. and Hitti, P. K.
1956   "Arabia", Article in the *Encyclopedia Britannica*; vol.2,p.188.

Religion in the Christian "Syrian-American Community"

PHILIP M. KAYAL

Unfortunately, contemporary academic interest in American ethnicity has ignored those groups which are either small in size (Armenians, Greeks, Lithuanians), politically unpopular (Syrians, Egyptians), or ideologically distinct (Russians, Ukrainians, and other 'Slovacks'). By focusing on the role of religious institutionalism on the formation, solidarity, structure and assimilation of the Arabic speaking Christian community, an important hiatus in the literature will be partially filled. More particularly, our concern will be with the function of religion in the acculturation and subsequent assimilation of American Eastern rite Catholics (Melkites and Maronites) of Syrian (Lebanese) ancestry. Indeed, the transformation of identities characteristic of this population is a consequence of the external relationships the collectivity's religious institutions have established with their American counterparts.

Christians in the Middle East, it must be remembered, traditionally defined themselves as members of "religious nations" rather than citizen/members of secular states. Assimilation, then, would commence after a new identity emerged here which was recognizeable to the host society. These Arabic speaking Christians had to become another "ethnic" group before they could assimilate. Yet, in so doing their own indigeneous religious rites had to become supporters and maintainers of their developing "Arab-cul-

true religion." Their "operative faith," (Herberg: 1960) became Arab-American culture. Unfortunately, sharing the same culture did not allow or prepare them for effective integration with other Arabic-speaking peoples of different religious traditions.

Arabic speaking Christian Americans:

Nearly ninety (90%) percent of all Arabic speaking immigrants arriving here before 1924 were Syrian Christians from the mountains of "the Lebanon" and the cities of Syria who were either Roman Catholics of Eastern rite or Syrian (Eastern) Orthodox Christians. Eastern Christianity, having developed in regional and rather provincial cultures, is composed of religious groups which are primarily of these two complementary traditions. For the first 1000 years of Christian history, both these religions shared the same deposit of faith with differences existing only in emphasis. (Congar: 1957).

The word 'Catholic,' which means universal and not uniform, is technically a misnomer when applied solely to the Roman tradition (rite) of the West since it ignores the other traditions of the East which when taken collectively constitute the totality of Catholic Christian history. Since the most popular Christian tradition in the East to develop did so in and around Constantinople, it became known as the Byzantine rite or tradition and Byzantium became considered the center of Eastern Christendom. In time, however, differences in opinion developed between this church and that of Rome.

The result was the Great Schism of 1054 which effectively severed Eastern Byzantine Christianity from Western Latin Christianity. The Catholic Church was split asunder and today we have two traditions coming from the same past—the Western and Eastern with the main point of disagreement being the definition of what Papal infallibility really consists of. The Catholic Church essentially became a western phenomenon with its Latin or Roman rite dominating there. Nevertheless, in the early 18th century, several communities of the Eastern Orthodox faith re-united themselves with the Church at Rome. They were commonly called "uniates." The most important group to do so were the Melkites of Syria. Since their reunion with Rome in 1724, these Syrian Grec-

Catholiques (Roūm Katholeeks) now number approximately 400,000 leaving a mother Church—the Syrian Antiochian Orthodox Church—of 700,000.

The Maronites of Lebanon, another Eastern rite Catholic group, claim to have never been in schism with Rome and represent the largest Arabic speaking Eastern Catholic group with some 1,000,000 followers. They are not Byzantine in style, practice, inspiration or mentality but follow, in altered form, the traditions of the Christian Church as it developed in Antioch. In times of oppression, they would flee to the Lebanese mountains which became their permanent home by the time of the Crusades. Because of their large numbers and their desperate struggle for survival, the Maronites became guardians of the land known as "the Lebanon." Fighting for Maronite civil security became synonymous with freedom of the land. Their Christian faith brought them on the side of the Crusaders and consequently they became more vulnerable to western socio-political ideals and more importantly to their theology and spirituality. Maronites, Melkite Catholics and the Syrian Orthodox have had their share of quarrels but presently their hostilities are due to the tendency of the Maronites to favor the process of "Latinization" (which became confused in America with Americanization) rather than develop its own Eastern inheritance. The social order to Lebanon is essentially Western, and now its spiritual life is changing accordingly.

In addition to their religio-political squabbles, another source of dispute was the overall reaction of the Easterners to the West— especially the French Latins and Protestants who introduced, albeit indirectly, more than Western spirituality (Jurji: 1956). Although the French were also Westerners, they did not receive the same reception as the Protestants who came to proselytize centuries later. For political, social and religious reasons the French became the highly valued friends of the Orient giving them a basis for their nationalism and modernization. Being Catholics, however, they had their greatest influence on the Lebanese Christians. Hitti mentions that "of the contacts established by the Latins with the peoples of the Near East, those with the Maronites proved to be the most fruitful, the most enduring." (Hitti, 1957:320). The outcome of the French influence was the intertwining of the fate of the Maronites with that of the state of Lebanon. The "cause" of one became the "cause" of the other, making the history of the contemporary Maronites practically the history of Lebanon as well. It is significant that the Maronite Patriarch with a staff of Bishops went to the Paris Peace Conference of 1919 to plead and voice the national aspirations and political sentiments of the Christian Lebanese.

Since the Maronites were the first Middle Easterners in modern times to open significant relations with the West, it should be expected that they would be responsible for the "westernization of the Lebanon." Indeed, so close are their bonds with their national state that for all practical purposes they are the "national church" of Lebanon. The Maronites have also been defined as a "religo-national group of Syriac origin," (Gasperetti, 1948:i) the majority of whom inhabit the republic of Lebanon. Through migration, however, they have become dispersed throughout the Mediterranean and the New World. Yet the tie with Lebanon is hardly broken. Indeed, its people talk of two Lebanons: "Lebanon the resident (al-muqim), and Lebanon the emigrant (al-mugtarib), literally the resident abroad" (Hitti, 1957).

Basically, the Maronites are Syrians living chiefly in "the Lebanon," but are, nevertheless, of the same cultural and racial origins as the Syrian and Melkite Catholics. Their existence as a "separate nation," is chiefly due to their ecclesiastical origins which has resulted in a strong group consciousness which only persecution could have produced and nurtured. Attachment to the Roman See has been a cornerstone of their tradition and invariably has been a source of suffering for them. Their staunch Catholicism and unquestioning obedience to the Roman Curia has also impeded their relations with their fellow Christian and Moslem Easterners.

Lebanon, consequently, is the only nation in the Middle East with approximately half her population being Christian. The total population of the Middle East is roughly 125,000,000 people of whom not more than 9,000,000 are Christian. They constitute between 5% and 6.7% of the total population there. The Coptic Patriarchate in Egypt, which dates back to St. Mark the Evangelist, numbers almost 7,000,000 and forms a distinctive minority, yet, they are considered full and committed Egyptian nationals. Estimates of the Christian population of Syria range from 3% to 15% of a total population of 6,000,000 (Hakim, 1973; Malik, 1964). The Christians outside of Egypt, Syria and Lebanon constitute even smaller minorities as do Western Catholics and Protestant residents.

When the Ottomans conquered the Byzantine empire in 1453, Christianity ceased to be the moving force of the East. Christians eventually perceived it to their general advantage to migrate away from the area and did so at the turn of this century. Arabic speaking people and Christians in particular became increasingly aware of the social, geographical, and political fragmentation of their society and found religion to be at the root of the areas social disorganization. The reshuffling and creation of new political boundaries that took place after 1915—when the bulk of the migration to the New World had ended—neither could compensate for the centuries of religious bigotry experienced or create an integrated national consciousness among and between the regions' various socio-religious communities.

The Turkish presence further accentuated these differences. True to the motto "divide and conquer" they kept the Moslems and Christians at odds with each other and left the East peculiarly vulnerable to the imperialist tendencies of the various Western powers. Hoping to gain a foothold in the area, the French supported the Maronites and the Russians cultivated ties with the Greek Orthodox faithful whose religion they shared. The English often assisted the Melkites and Druse. The Turks, of course, did what they could to keep the Christian sects divided and hostile to one another and then proceeded to antagonize them collectively. They especially successful keeping the Melkite Catholics in constant conflict with the Syrian Orthodox even though these two groups shared the same history and tradition.

It is no wonder that the original Syrian immigrants here arrived here confused in terms of their identity. Indeed, the forebearers of today's "Lebanese-Americans" actually came here with Syrian passports even though they themselves felt that they owed their major allegiance neither to a secular state, region or culture, but to their "people" who were defined not as fellow nationals but as other Christians of the same tradition (rite). In no way were the early immigrants "Arabs" in the popular sense of the word. If anything, they strongly resisted being so classified, as Arab in their mind meant Moslem and hence oppressor. Nor were they Turks, Asians or Assyrians. Rather they were Semitic Christians who were Arab in culture and if they were Catholic, they were either Maronite Catholics from Mt. Lebanon or Byzantine-Melkite Catholics from the cities and towns of Syria. For the sake of historical accuracy, our use of the word "Syrian" will include all turn of the century immigrants from the modern nations of Jordan, Israel (Palestine), Lebanon or Syria who were either Melkites, Maronites or Syrian-Orthodox. Most Scholars agree that this was the custom of the immigrants themselves (Berger, 1958:314), i.e., to call themselves "Syrians."

It was only after the founding of the *Al-Hoda* press that a campaign, often times unsuccessful, was undertaken to make the "Syrians" recognize their "Lebanese origins" (Al-Hoda, 1968). Yet, the word "Lebanese" was never publicly used by any Arabic publication until 1930 *(The Syrian World,* 1930; Gibran, 1926; Mokarzel, 1927; Hitti, 1924; Yazbek, 1923).

Demographically speaking, it is true that most Arabic speaking Americans are descendants of "Lebanese" rather than Syrian immigrants. But any identity based on national or geographic boundaries was foreign to all the emigrants from the Middle East. Not only has the word "Syrian" been used to describe different regions and populations, it was purely a western invention which most of the immigrants were forced to use for the sake of their hosts who did not know how to classify them.

Dr. Philip K. Hitti (1957:476) of Princeton summarizes the point:

> While at home they thought of themselves as Beirutis, Zahlawis, Dayranis, Hasrunis, Haqilanis, or as Maronites, Druses, Greek-Orthodox, Matawilah, in their lands of emigration they had to answer the question "What are you?" in broader terms. Even then some replied "Suri" (Syrian).

Since identification in terms of national origin was not a strong tradition among them, they have been termed a "collectivity" rather than an ethnic group (Treudley, 1953:261-265). Nathan Glazer (1964:166) has written that the Syrians were immigrants "from areas outside the Western concepts of states and nations." This was because their unique religious history caused the various religious traditions to act primarily as if each were a different "ethnic group."

Consequently, their traditional identity patterns made it almost impossible for them to develop pan-Arabic organizations which could unify all those who spoke Arabic. The problem was complicated by the fact that most Arabic speaking Americans have come to consider themselves "Lebanese-Christians" and hence committed to Western socio-political forms. In a sense, the Moslem governments of Syria, Jordan, Palestine and Egypt have reinforced their separateness by making Arab nationalism their particular monopoly and by reminding the Christians that they are westerners in reality and hence anti-Arab.

This situation has been termed the "Levantine Dilemma," (Malik, 1964) and is particularly acute for the French speaking Lebanese. The conflict is a result of the need to fuse westernization with Arab culture and history. The Moslems see westernization as progress plus de-Arabization and point to both modern Lebanon and Israel as an example of the consequence of such adaptations. The Lebanese reaction, however, must be viewed as a conscious attempt to stay Christian in a sea of Islam and Eastern Catholics in a sea of Roman Catholicism. Malik, (1964:89) writes

> Their entire attitude and mentality reflect this minority consciousness. The Lebanese Christians are only a partial exception, because they too, when they mentally set themselves politically within the context of the larger Muslim world of the Near East to which they belong, automatically fall into the strange unauthentic workings of the minority mind. The Christians of the Near East develop a dual soul, with a terrific inner tension, often also exceedingly comic, and they suffer under a pathetic sense of insecurity. They will not let go their Christianity, but at the same time they must do nothing that will offend their Muslim world. They do not want to betray their Christian heritage, but neither do they want to prove traitorous to the Muslim world to which they belong economically, socially, and politically.

This deterioration and rape of Arab culture can only be reversed, according to Arab scholar A. H. Hourani (1946:70-71) by the Arabs believing "in their own possibilities and their own power, given the necessary conditions of building up once more a world of thought and activity which they can call their own and through which they can make their contribution to the world's civilization." The "modern" western state of Israel (created by the West and reflective of its values), therefore, carved out of the authentically Arab community of Palestine, becomes the focus of conflicts in a region already torn by the demands of social change.

In America, the problem of "Levantism" is no less severe. Only now it is more complicated. In the first place, the pro-Western Christian Lebanese prefer not to be identified or involved with the pro-Eastern Syrian Christians. Secondly, the Maronite Lebanese tend to favor "latinization" (Americanization) and the Melkite Syrians have begun to restress their unique Byzantine heritage. Thirdly, both groups have never considered themselves Arabs and fought consistently against being so labelled. On the other hand, the emphasis today is on being "Arab" and other immigrants (Palestinians, Egyptians) arriving from the Middle East have no real difficulty relating to this category. The original Syrian-Lebanese immigrants, however, do and usually do not perceive the new arrivals as potential members of their communities. Since the historical realities of the Middle East only changed recently—after the migration here—the Christian Syrian and Lebanese Americans have not been prepared for active involvement with other Arabic speaking Americans simply because they share the same culture.

Even the objective goal of reclaiming Palestine is beyond their range of historical experience and is in reality a problem only for a localized Arabic speaking population. Arabic culture, here or abroad, has not been able to politically or socially unify its bearers in any singular effort. This might be due to the fact that "Arab" is now a cultural term and not an ethnic-racial one. If anything, Arabs are a small if not extinct minority. Any "Arab" cause would have to be transnational and assume the awareness of being Arab first and Jordanian, Syrian, Lebanese, Morrocan, Egyptian, etc. second. Willingness to do so is hardly evident in the Middle East and is not even desired by most of their American counterparts.

Moreover, historical and participational identification patterns are overlapped for most Middle Easterners, i.e., they have effectively limited the boundaries of psycho-social identification and responsibility to those of the same family. Since the Middle Easterner sees his family as an extension of himself and his "religion" or rite as a continuation of his family, social life rarely existed beyond the extended clan which more or less was religiously ("ritually") homogeneous. The village represented the ultimate limit for secondary social discourse, but a sense of peoplehood and belonging is reserved to the family which is made up of co-religionists (Tannous, 1942).

This situation is essentially duplicated in the cities of the Middle East. Syrian towns were often divided into districts inhabited by particular religious and ethnic groups. There was little sense of real identification within the larger community. Individuals were identified by their "quarters," creating an aura of mistrust between the segments (Hourani, 1947:63-67). Consequently, the Syrians have never really gotten over their distrust of one another and hence their ability to develop viable political and social institutions outside of the religious sphere has been seriously hampered. Their collective individualism and social provincialism has meant political impotence and indifference in this country.

Since families were religiously homogeneous, family loyalty became translated into religious fidelity. The Syrian is the man "without a country par excellence," his patriotism thus takes the form of love for family and religion (Hitti, 1924:25 & 26). For all practical purposes, his church takes the place of the state for him. All cooperation between individuals, therefore, is centered around his traditional groups—family, village and religion.

It was no wonder then, that the original organizations of the Syrian Christian immigrants reflected these divisions. When the Syrians "sought out the company and aid of his fellows," (Handlin, 1959:76) he invariably thought of those from his home town. Speaking of the Syrians in 1924, Hitti notes that membership in organizations were always based on some geographical and religious distinction (Hitti, 1924:30).

This provincialism in thinking is also reflected in the Syrian Christian attitude towards naturalization a process and state of

being he could not understand (Houghton 1911), and which language identity could not help. If immigrants named themselves by
their language and learned to identify themselves in national terms
by it (Handlin, 1951:186-187), the Syrian could do no such thing
for he spoke "Arabic" not "Syrian," while not being an Arab or at
least not wishing to be identified as such. There seems to be some
inconclusive evidence that language and culture united the Syrians
over and above religious differences. Oscar Handlin believes that
"a common medium of communication made them readers of the
same newspapers and eventually brought them together in a
'United Syrian Organization'" (Handlin, 1954:67). Culture,
however, in no way brought them together in the manner suggested. No common institutional integration took place until relatively recently and the existence of any such organization has not
been uncovered by this researcher. Culture, as we are attempting to
demonstrate, did allow the various Christian sects to mix socially on
superficial levels but did not succeed in creating a common ethnic
consciousness.

Rarely, if ever, had meaningful identification with national
boundaries or racial origins been achieved. Even national governments existed to protect the collective rights of each of the Christian sects, the Moslems and Jews (Swartz, 1970), who traditionally
had a given status before the law and relationship to the total society. There was a unity in culture, language, moral code, art and
music, but not a common history or social past. Religious differences seemed to always interfere with any sense of common nationalism. Indeed, religion more or less divided   the Middle
Easterner into two generally antagonistic camps: Christian and
Moslem. Christianity was further subdivided into several mutually
jealous and hostile communities based on ecclesiastical tradition or
rite. Similar sectarian differences also existed in the Muslim community.

The ruling and oppressive Turkish powers, who had to integrate
a heterogeneous population, capitalized on the Christian diversity
by playing each 'sect' against one another and by structuring each
Christian tradition (rite) into a "millet" which was really a church
organized into a nationality as well as a nationality organized into a

church. In his analysis of this phenomenon, sociologist Werner Cahnman (1944:526) writes:

> The Millet may be defined as the peculiar political organization which gave to non-Moslem subjects of the Ottoman Empire the right to organize their communities possessing delegated political power under their own ecclesiastical chiefs. In matters affecting the community, the government treated it as a whole unit dealing with its leaders rather than individual members. The head of the millet was directly responsible to the state for the administration of all its subjects. Although the millet lacked territorial cohesion and military power and had, therefore, to be protected by the ruling warrior class, it formed in many respects an autonomous unit within the state. Yet, the members of the millet were limited in their general citizenship by virtue of the very fact that the laws of personal statute were based on religious sanctions.

That these "rites" became "nations" stemmed from the original confusion in the Turkish mind between religion and race. The Turk had the erroneous idea that the differences of religion in his empire could be explained by the "fact" that each group is descended from a race which once held that particular religion. Since so much civil law, and the state of each subject in temporal matters, depend on the religious body to which he belongs, the Christians have begun to look upon themselves as different nations in the ordinary sense of the word. But when they talk of their "nation" meaning their church, they do not realize that this is a purely artificial use of the word introduced by the Moslems because they had no other way of classifying them.

Their Encounter with America

Because of the organizational mode used in the Middle East which inextricably intertwined the family system with the religious (the latter supplying the socio-political reality and the sense of peoplehood), the "Syrian-American collectivity" would not easily emerge as a single, integrated ethnic community. In fact, there are in this country, three distinct yet interrelated Syrian identity groups—Melkites, Maronites and Syrian-Orthodox—which when taken together make up the Syrian-American community. For all practical purposes, this situation reduces the functional importance of the "collectivity" to a general and diffuse level.

"Syrian" becomes a term, which Teudley (1953:261) suggests, "labels the category which is to be dealt with but does not indicate the source or the sense of belongingness which makes an individual a member of the collectivity. Geography supplies only the framework within which sociological analysis is applied." Assimilation for the Syrians, then, would result in interior structural changes which would themselves be a consequence of the types of accommodation offered them by America's religious institutions. It was this encounter which taught the Melkites how to coexist with the Maronites and Syrian-Orthodox who were all antagonistic to one another. Adaptation to the outside world forced a re-organization of communal priorities and encouraged the decline of religious distinctiveness and separateness.

The process began in the religious sphere. As Raymond Breton (1964:193) notes, "some of the most crucial factors bearing on the absorption of immigrants would be in the social organization of the communities which the immigrant contacts in the receiving country." Since the only "parallel institution" belonging to the Syrians which was different from the publicly sanctioned ways of the larger population was their church, and since "religious institutions have the greatest effect in keeping the immigrants' personal associations within the boundaries of the ethnic community," (Breton, 1963:200), it would be in this area that they would most experience the tensions of assimilation. Arab historian Philip K. Hitti (1924:121) predicted the outcome some fifty years ago. "The more the immigrants," he wrote, "enter into the religious life of America, the better and quicker they become Americans."

For all practical purposes, then, assimilation for the Syrians meant their integration into the traditional institutional religions of American society. The Catholic Syrians thus found their most serious integration conflict with American Latin rite Catholicism which was culturally and institutionally dominated by the English-speaking Irish. Since it was always possible for all western-rite

Catholics "to share the Mass," it was through this common vehicle that an integrated American Catholic institutional life emerged.

However, the Syrians came from the Christian East. Hence, they would be socially and religiously marginal to this development. In the first place, their churches and parishes were inclusive to a degree unmatched by other Catholic groups. Secondly, as Eastern Catholics, they differed in their interpretation of Christian cosmology and morality. Thirdly, their symbols and liturgical systems were different from those commonly used and understood in the West, and the structure of their parishes and dioceses varied accordingly. (Harte & Nuesse, 1951: Warner & Srole, 1945). Finally, there were also differences in religious discipline, e.g. a married clergy was accepted and commonplace.

Because of centuries of conditioning, the American Catholic hierarchy with encouragement and direction from the Oriental Congregation in Rome responded in typical Roman fashion to the legitimate claims of the emerging American Eastern Catholic population. The situation was further complicated by the particular problems facing an assimilating and emerging American Catholic Church which felt it to be in the best interests of an "American Church" to render these strange Catholics (or Uniates) peripheral to Catholic life and to reduce them to another Catholic ethnic group which would be Americanized and/or "latinized" in time.

For the latin rite Irish, the Syrians were merely another ethnic group which disrupted and discredited a church which was trying so desperately to be American and unified. Thus, their desire for ecclesiastical independence became confused in the minds of the Latins with "Cahenslyism;" the government of their churches with "Trusteeism;" and their married clergy with Protestantism. More importantly they feared that the Easterners would disrupt the "universality" of the Catholic Church which was narrowly defined at that time as uniformity and conformity. The Syrian confrontation was more than just ethnic conflict: it was rather a confrontation between two religious disciplines, two ecclesiologies and two religio-cultural traditions which never fully understood one another.

Because they valued their Catholic heritage, the Syrians allowed themselves to become a latinized Catholic ethnic group rather than force American Catholicism to be legitimately pluralistic in terms of rite, language and liturgy. In turn, they not only gained access to the channels of social acceptance and upward mobility, but resolved their primary "culture conflict" here which arose out of their inherent deviancy, i.e., non-conformity to the expected religious practices of the American Church. According to the first American born Melkite priest ordained here:

> They wanted to be more "American" in all aspects of the word. Americanization remoulded home, family, work and recreation. Some unfortunately, overzealous in their good intentions, confused the word "Americanization" with "Latinization." The general idea seemed to be, "We are in America now—therefore, our churches and customs should be the same as those of the other American Catholics (Latins); so that we may all be alike; we should not confuse people." (Maloof, 1951:261).

Their orientation in the religious life reflected quite accurately their attitude and approach to American society in general, i.e., it complemented their tendency to seek rather than avoid some form of effective integration with American society—especially in religious terms. They wanted to be Americans of "the Catholic kind" no matter what the cost would be to their communal life. Melkite and Maronite latinization, then, helped them keep their community together by warding off those difficulties which could have emerged from a too rapid secular assimilation without a parallel adjustment in the religious sphere. In altering their basic religious identities, they were forced to find a reasonable substitute which they did by becoming, for a time, "Syrians" in the ethnic sense.

Consequently, they proceeded to modify their rite and the symbols of their "corporate identity" to be more American. In so doing, however, they effectively (albeit unwillingly) destroyed the basis for a separate and meaningful communal life. Essentially, they made boundary maintenance impractical and almost impossible. Either they could participate in an unauthentic and latinized Eastern Church or simply become Latin rite Catholics by supporting those churches and incorporating themselves into their social and religious life.

In fact, the Syrian Eastern Catholics lost over half of their faithful to the Latin or American rite. While the official estimates of the Melkite and Maronite Exarchates place their numbers at 50,000 and 100,000 respectively, there are less than 20,000 Melkites registered in the 25 Melkite "parishes" of the United States. A greater number, estimated at 30,000 are only nominally Melkite, practically Latin. (Elya, 1965: 1) The Maronites, on the other hand, who have over 40 parishes claim to have 100,000 "active Maronites" and estimate their "loss to other rites" as 50,000. (Maronite Exarchate (Prot. #50/69).

More importantly, an intensive study of the Brooklyn Melkite community completed in 1964 reveals that 46% of the second generation of canonical Melkites actually identified with the Latin rite and considered themselves Latins with the proportion increasing to 55% by the third generation. (Kayal, 1970: Chapter 10)

Coming from a powerless and subdued socio-religious tradition, lacking any substantial and appreciative awareness of their own past, and being unable to organize themselves into a workable and acceptable identity without radically altering their traditional patterns, they were literally overwhelmed by the Latins. This was more a result of the material and social appeal of Latin Christianity than its religious and salvific significance. As in Syria, the Eastern rites became looked down upon as being for "mere peasants." The Latin rite stands for European and Christian civilization and influence; for its attractive ideas of progress, for prestige, education, commerce, for being "in" with the French and with the West. (Atwater, 1935: 18). In the Syrian immigrants' mind, to be modern, affluent and American meant to be Latin.

Their flirtation with the Latin rite was a consequence of their general shortage of educated and informed priests to direct them, lack of a unified diocesan organization, their widespread dispersal throughout the country, their unwillingness or inability to build their own schools and finally their general middle class status. Yet, the primary factor influencing the direction that the Syrian

Catholic community took in its attempts at survival was the unwillingness of American Catholicism to accept an "autonomous" Eastern American Catholicism as valid and legitimate and the desire of the Syrians themselves to be "acculturated" without being completely assimilated. Since American Catholic society was more willing to accept cultural plurality (since it was temporary) but not a plurality of rites the Syrians began to "latinize" their churches for acceptance.

This accommodation was especially important for the Melkites and differed in causation from the Maronites who had always imitated Latin customs because of the prestige that being like the West gave them. The Melkites, on the other hand, were Syrians and because their rite was so distinctive, they were assumed to be Moslem! When it was proven that they were Christian, they were thought to be Eastern Orthodox not "Uniates." Desiring not to be recognized as Orthodox, they changed their rites and traditions to "American" (Latin) usuage, and propelled their numerous lay elites into the ranks of Catholic society.

No one perceived it as problematic that "so many" of these lay leaders were positioned not because of demonstrated leadership, knowledge or administrative ability in religious terms, but because of economic achievement and generosity towards the Latin hierarchs—the very group which oppressed them. To be recognized by the Latin Diocese as an important Catholic philanthropist affected the sponsoring community in at least two ways. First, it achieved for the sponsors a certain amount of recognition from American Catholic "society" at the same time that it supplied them with recognizeable and obviously acceptable leaders; and secondly, it reflected on the Catholicity of the whole Melkite and Maronite community from which they came.

If the influence of the Catholic elites was to bring them and the groups they represented into the consciousness of American Catholicism, they also helped to alter their rites to make them more acceptable to the dominant society. It can also be argued that latinization or the process of accommodation to American society was merely the religious equivalent of a rapid integration into the culture and life style of the American middle-class. Assimilation in economic terms was simply a one generation phenomenon for these Syrian-Lebanese, i. e., it was the immigrant generation which more or less accumulated the wealth which was sustained by their children and used to bring them into even wider contact with American society. While various studies on the Syrian-Americans allude to their mobility, wealth, occupational diversity, only two studies offer any statistical data.

In a sample study of the Syrians of Springfield, Mass., N. Aruri (1969:51-66) notes that a very distinctive characteristic of this heavily Maronite community is the relatively high percentage (74%) of self-employed and owners or part-owners of a business. " . . . today, the grandchildren of the immigrants are moving rapidly into the professional and other enterprises requiring special skills such as manufacturing, insurance and real estate, etc."

Information on the Christian Lebanese community of Los Angeles, California reveals that there is a "preponderant number of individuals who work in, or own, market stores, cocktail lounges, restaurants, nightclubs and dry goods stores, retail and/or wholesale. Also the large number of professional persons listed is striking. (Dlin, 1961: 21). Writing in 1946, Habib Katibah notes that by then "Syrians had entered completely the mainstream of economic and social life, being represented in practically every industry and profession open to all Americans." (Katibah, 1964: 284). This especially was the accomplishment of the children of the "factory and mill workers" (the children of the entrepreneurs, while being educated, tended to remain in the family enterprises), who because of the frugality and temperance of their parents were propelled educationally and hence occupationally into the American middle class.

If assimilation can be considered completed when intermarriage takes place on an intensive scale, (Kennedy, 1944: 13; Marcson 1950: 75-78), then the best indice of Syrian mobility and integration into American life is their out-marriage rates with children of "non-Arabic speaking Americans." The following data draws a distinction between those between two Arabs (Homogeneous) and those which involve only a Melkite boy or Melkite girl. Since Melkites are Syrians, the data might reflect marriage trends among the non-Melkite Christian Syrian-Lebanese population since they would constitute the Arab population the Melkites married into when in a homogeneous union.

TABLE I

Comparative Table of Intermarriages in the Melkite Parishes of Boston, Massachusettes; Brooklyn, New York; Central Falls, Rhode Island; Cleveland, Ohio; Danbury, Connecticut; Lawrence, Massachusettes; New London, Connecticut; Paterson, New Jersey; Worcester, Massachusetts.

| | 1954 | | | | 1957 | | | | 1961 | | | |
	T.	*Ho.*	*Hu.*	*W.*	*T.*	*Ho.*	*Hu.*	*W.*	*T.*	*Ho.*	*Hu.*	*W.*
Boston	7	3	3	1	8	4	3	1	9	6	0	3
Brklyn.	24	14	6	4	27	10	14	3	24	8	14	2
C. Falls	—	—	—	—	—	—	—	—	13	2	5	6
Clvlnd.	2	2	0	0	13	6	4	3	4	1	2	1
Danbury	3	2	1	0	2	1	0	1	5	0	5	0
Lawrence	10	2	6	2	6	2	4	0	9	2	5	2
N. London	—	—	—	—	—	—	—	—	1	0	0	1
Paterson	19	3	8	8	15	3	8	4	13	2	5	6
Worcester	4	2	1	1	4	2	1	1	1	0	0	1
TOTALS:	69	28	25	16	75	28	34	13	79	21	36	22
PERCENT:	40%				37%				26%			

| | 1963 | | | | 1964 | | | | 1968 | | | |
	T.	*Ho.*	*Hu.*	*W.*	*T.*	*Ho.*	*Hu.*	*W.*	*T.*	*Ho.*	*Hu.*	*W.*
Boston	12	6	1	5	12	2	5	5	17	2	4	11
Brklyn.	20	6	10	4	29	7	18	4	22	4	14	4
C. Falls	11	3	2	6	9	1	5	3	—	—	—	—
Clvlnd.	7	3	3	1	8	2	4	2	7	3	3	1
Danbury	9	2	6	1	2	0	1	1	—	—	—	—
Lawrence	6	0	4	2	12	2	7	3	19	3	10	6
N. London	3	0	1	2	5	0	3	2	—	—	—	—
Paterson	15	3	5	7	22	3	11	8	25	1	13	11
Worcester	3	0	3	0	8	0	4	4	—	—	—	—
TOTALS:	86	23	35	28	107	17	58	32	90	13	44	33
PERCENT:	26%				15%				14%			

T. — Total Mariages
Ho. — Homogeneous (Both are of Arabic speaking Origin)
Hu. — Husband only (is of Arabic Speaking Origin)
W. — Wife only (is of Arabic Speaking Origin)
Percent—Percentage of Homogeneous marriages compared to the total of marriages registered in the Church

Syrian out-marriages (at least among the Melkites) have been high for nearly three decades. Data collected for a 1964-65 study reveals that only 17 couples out of 107 (less than 15%) married in the Melkite Church were both of Arabic-speaking origin. In 1953, only 5 marriages out of 15 (33%) in St. Ann's Melkite Church, Paterson, N.J. were homogeneous. By 1968, only one marriage out of 35 (.028%) were between two Syrians.[1] The Syrian community, then, would loose all its mixed offspring if the churches adhered to a strict Arabic tradition. The Syrian population in any given area is usually too small to reproduce itself by in-marriage. The churches would only have the in-married population affiliated with them if they had not latinized and Americanized themselves. Latinization allowed the out-married couple to, at least, affiliate with the churches and Americanization allowed them to do so in non-ethnic terms. It can also be argued that latinization also encouraged out-marrying. In either case, the community would be substantially weakened.

American Syrianisms

By changing their external religious symbols, the Syrian Catholics effectively altered the interior life which these symbols should have reflected. In one sense, this accommodation lessened the possibility and speed of group dissolution. In another, it accelerated it by dynamically affecting the organization and function of the total community. With religious differences being neutralized, they could now at least mix socially with all other Syrians who were also interested in creating and sustaining a way of life which was socially inclusive yet culturally non-offensive to American society.

They created a way of life based on selected Arabic cultural traits which we can term 'American Syrianisms' which all of the community's religious institutions supported. Indeed, their churches would become the vehicle of its development. We cite especially the Maronite tradition because it so singularly intertwined an ethnic culture with a religious tradition. Ascribing to the philosophy that "our Lebanese community is supported by our culture and religion . . . both of them reflecting our soul and spirit . . ." (Maloof, 1958: 283), the Maronite Church here has become the primary bearer and preserver of "Arabic culture," as interpreted by Lebanon, rather than the reflection of a "universal" Catholic Eastern Rite, which could be open to all ethnics.

Catholic Syrian-Americans opted for an "ethnic-identity" at a time when most ethnic groups seemed to be "melting" into a 'triple-melting pot' of religion. The Eastern Orthodox Syrians also had to accommodate themselves to the changing interests and needs of their "Americanizing" constitutency until that time when a unified (together with Greeks and Russians, etc.) American Orthodox Church restressing faith emerged. Neither group believed that their church or community could survive and grow without an Arab population involved in it. They tended to place in-marriage with other Christian "wlad Arab" in a primary position.

Catholics and Orthodox were thus brought together over the ethnic-cultural and in-marriage issue, and the perplexing question of how to acculturate without assimilating into oblivion. A corollary dilemma they shared was how to free their churches from dependence on ethnicity for survival which is generally considered necessary to ward off rejection by the second and third generation.

Regardless of the specific content of the ethnic tradition, Marshall Sklare (1957: 459-463) tells us that these ethnic churches became transferred or operated under the guise of "religious distinctiveness" which, unlike ethnic separateness, has always been the esteemed form of American diversity. The churches, thus, came to share the additional task of preserving a particular sub-culture and ethnic history.

Sharing a common culture actually became the basis for community since it made available a common value system and allowed expectations for interpersonal behavior to be fulfilled. Culture eventually neutralized their religious divisiveness and helped answer the changing social needs of their emerging community. In commenting on the effects of having a commonly shared culture in a structurally splintered ethnic group, priest-sociologist Constantine Volaitas (1961: 72) succinctly summarizes the situation at hand:

> The Syrian community still maintains a strong extended kinship system even though marked by separation into Orthodox,

Catholic and Protestant divisions. The important factor is identifying with the Syrian community as a whole and especially with the larger family group from which one descends. Many Syrian parishes are practically a kinship system in themselves with almost everyone related in one way or another.

Since the Syrians concentrated institutionally on building their churches which became the focal points for most of their social, cultural, religious and interpersonal activities, being identified as Syrian-American meant being identified with one of its religious traditions. It is to be either a Syrian-Orthodox, Maronite or Melkite Catholic. Conversely, association with one of these churches means being engulfed in a network of "refined" Arabic culture. The primary interest and function of the churches became attracting the American born Syrians simply because they were all "wlad Arab," (Children of the Arab East) and not because they had a religious obligation to serve a distinct community of believers.

Nevertheless, they never overcame their religious biases completely. Socially, they continued the patterns of the old country which meant primarily relating to only those who could be considered extensions of the family. According to Treudley, (1953: 261) "only Christians . . . are considered to be our kind of people." Moslems, Arabic speaking Jews and Arabs in general are excluded from the in-group. "Furthermore," she continues, "membership is felt to rest not so much on the country of origin as on the biological position of the individual. The collectivity is less a nationality group to the ordinary person than a union of extended kinships."

The extension of social intercourse from those of the same family and rite to those of the same religion and then to those of the same faith was incomplete, i.e., it never reached fruition in an overall commitment to Arab culture and its people. Religion again became the extent of their nationality or ethnic identification. Treudley (263) writes, "Some parents choose to mate their daughters within their own faith, even if it means going outside the collectivity, but they seem to be exceptions to the general rule. Most parents prefer to have their children leave the church rather than cross nationality lines."

This was all made possible when all the churches in question could offer their communicants an abbreviated form of Arab culture. "Syrianisms" notes Treudley (262) "had a simple meaning: food habits, crafts, music and dancing, the rites of hospitality, authoritarian family patterns, the closeness and warmth of family ties, a religious ritual with many common features, whether the church was Maronite, Melkite or Eastern Orthodox."

In another revealing passage, she refers to the overall integration of these "Syrianisms" with American culture.

> The collectivity is most responsive to the intermingling of American and Syrian symbolism . . . American culture provides the formal ends for such an organization and techniques for their achievement, while Syrian culture adds the colorful dances and pagentry that make for vivid enjoyment. (265)

This integration was facilitated by the overall social disposition of the Syrian population. Syrian values, it seems, never really had to be modified and culture conflict was never an important issue. Berger (1958-316) states quite categorically that

> Even while they were still in the lower income brackets and in working class occupations the "Syrians" displayed the social characteristics of the middle classes in American urban centers. Studies of these Arab immigrants in Chicago, Pittsburgh and the South reveal a common pattern: low crime rate, better than average health, High I. Q.'s and more regular school attendance among the children, few intermarriages and divorce.

Outside the religious sphere, then, the Syrians' adaptation was not very dramatic and was facilitated by their churches themselves. They were thus spared the wholesale rejection of ethnicity supposedly characteristic of all second generation Americans. The immigrants' children could not reject what their own forebears modified or return to that which his predecessors never fully rejected. Dual life styles, consequently, are available to the Syrian-Americans. In private, social discourse, they could be 'selectively' ethnic and in public life fully American—a situation which was necessitated by their rapid integration into the national economy (Kayal, 1970: Chap. 6).

The Syrian-American Christian "community", then, is a voluntary form of association with a network of cultural traits which are essentially American in addition to those modified Arabic customs which evolve around food, music and folk dancing. It is a community characterized by weakened interest and ties to the rest of the Arab world and to the Palestinian question. It is an American creation, born out of the conflict generated by the need to have an acceptable identity in a pluralistic society.

The members lack a common secular history and because they are essentially confused over the question of identity, they have not been able to institutionalize the objective of maintaining their ethnic community with total success. The rise of the Lebanese "nationality" controversy has not clarified the situation. In light of the evidence, the community must now find other reasons for expecting in-group solidarity and participation among their American born children, or perhaps recombine their identification with other Arabic-speaking groups. An impetus to do so may come from the recent rise of ethnic identifications noticeable in American culture today.

NOTES

[1]Data taken from an unpublished, research report prepared by Rev. John Elya and cited earlier. Data from 1965 onward was collected by this writer.

REFERENCES

Al-Hoda
  1968   *The Story of Lebanon and Its Emigrants Taken from the Newspaper Al-Hoda.* New York: Al-Hoda.

Aruri, Naseer II.
  1969   "The Arab-American Community of Springfield; Mass.," in Hagopian, Elaine and Ann Paden, *The Arab-Americans: Studies in Assimilation.* Illinois: Medina Univ. Press.

Atwater, Donald
  1935   *Catholic Eastern Churches.* Wisconsin: Bruce.

Berger, Morroe
  1958   "America's Syrian Community." *Commentary,* Vol. 25, #4 (April) 314-323

Breton, Raymond
    1964   "Institutional Completeness of Ethnic Communities and the Personal Relations of Immigrants, "*American Journal of Sociology*, Vol. 70, #2 (September) 193-205

Cahnman, Werner
    1944   "Religion and Nationality," *American Journal of Sociology*, Vol. 49, #6 (May) 524-529

Congar, Yves
    1957   *After Nine Hundred Years*. New York: Fordham University Press.

Dlin, Norman
    1961   Some Cultural and Geographical Aspects of the Christian Lebanese In Metropolitan Los Angeles, Masters Thesis: Univ. of California.

Elya, John Fr.
    1965   "The Accommodation of a Socio-Religious Sub-System: The Melkite Catholics in the United States," Unpublished term report: Boston College.

Gasperetti, Eli
    1948   The Maronites: The Origin and Development of a Theocracy. Unpublished Master's Dissertation, Columbia University.

Gibran, Kalil
    1926   "Gibran's Message to Young Americans of Syrian Origin," *The Syrian World*, 1:1 (July) 4-5.

Glazer, Nathan
    1964   "Ethnic Groups in America: From National Culture to Ideology," in Berger, Abel, *et al.*, *Freedom and Control in Modern Society*. New York: Octagon Books.

Hakim, Patriarch George
    1973   "His Beatitude Patriarch Maximos V In America," *Sophia* Vol. 3 #3, pp. 1-4.

Handlin, Oscar
    1951   *The Uprooted*. Boston: Little, Brown and Co.

    1954   *The American People In the Twentieth Century*. Cambridge: Harvard University Press.

1959   *Immigration as a Factor in American Life*. Englewood Cliffs: Prentice-Hall

Harte, Thomas and C. J. Nuesse
1951   *The Sociology of the Parish*. Milwaukee: Bruce

Herberg, Will
1960   *Protestant, Catholic, Jew*. New York: Doubleday & Co.

Hitti, Philip K.
1924   *Syrians in America*. New York: Doran Co.

Hitti, Philip K.
1957   *Lebanon In History*. New York: MacMillan Co.

Houghton, Louise
1911   "Syrians in the United States," *The Survey*, Vol. 26, July 1; Aug. 5; Sept. 2nd; October 7th.

Hourani, A. H.
1946   *Syria and Lebanon*. London: Oxford University Press

Jurji, Edward
1956   *The Middle East: Its Religion and Culture*. Philadelphia: Westminister Press

Katibah, Habib
1946   *Arabic-Speaking Americans* (Pamphlet) New York: The Institute of Arab-American Affairs.

Kayal, Philip M.
1970   The Churches of the Catholic Syrians and Their Role in the Assimilation Process, New York: Fordham University. Unpublished Doctoral Dissertation, 71-8721.

Kennedy, Ruby Jo
1944   "Single or Triple Melting Pot?" *American Journal of Sociology*, 49:4, (January), 331-339.

Malik, Charles H.
1964   "The Near East," in Miner Searle Bates and Wilhelm Pauck, *The Prospects of Christianity Throughout the World*. New York: Charles Scribner.

Maloof, Rev. Allen
1951   "Catholics of the Byzantine-Melkite Rite in the United States of America," *Eastern Churches Quarterly*. Winter, 1951, #5.

Maloof, Louis
   1958   A Sociological Study of Arabic Speaking People in Mexico.
           Unpublished Ph. D. dissertation, University of Florida.

Marcson, Simon
   1950   "A Theory of Intermarriage and Assimilation," *Social Forces*,
           29:1 (October), 75-78.

Maronite Exarchate
   1969   Prot. #50/69.

Mokarzel, Salloum
   1927   "History of the Syrians in New York," *New York American*,
           October 3.

Newsweek
   1968   "Brazil: Sons of the Phoenicians," January 8th. p. 40.

Sklare, Marshall
   1957   "The Function of Ethnic Churches: Judaism in the United
           States," in J.M. Yinger, *Religion, Society and the Individual*.
           New York: Macmillan Co. 459-463.

Swartz, Merlin
   1970   "The Position of Jews in Arab Lands Following the Rise of
           Islam," *The Moslem World*, LX, #1.

Tannous, Afif
   1942   "Group Behavior in the Village Community of Lebanon,"
           American Journal of Sociology 48:2; pp. 231-239.

The Syrian World
   1930   "Lebanese-American Festival," Vol. 5, #1, 52-53.

Treudley, Mary Bosworth
   1953   "The Ethnic Group as a Collectivity," *Social Forces*, 31:3
           (March), 261-265.

Yazbek, Msgr. Joseph
   1923   "The Syrians," in C. E. McGuire, *Catholic Builders of the
           Nation*. Boston: Continental Press, Inc.

Zelditch, Morris
   1936   The Syrians in Pittsburgh, Unpublished Master's Dissertation:
           University of Pittsburgh.

The Detroit Maronite Community

May Ahdab-Yehia

Despite the increasing literature on ethnic groups, very few writers have been interested in the relatively small wave of "Arab" migrants who arrived on the American continent toward the end of the nineteenth century. The Maronites, primarily a Lebanese ethno-religious community, was one of the smallest but earliest Arab group to migrate to the United States. Tracing the origin of their ancestors to their patron St Maron who founded the community around the year 400 A.D. (Salibi. 1962:6), ten of thousands of these Lebanese Catholics headed toward the United States, Canada, Mexico and the rest of the American continent during the later half of the nineteenth century, seeking higher social status or attracted by the economic and work opportunities of the new world (Suleiman. 1967:11, 12, 13).

Through the centuries, the political realities of the Middle East have led to an interwining of religious and national loyalties. The Maronites, a Catholic Eastern rite group, can thus be conceived of as a nationality group which for historical reasons are mostly located in Lebanon, a nation that obtained its independence from the French in 1943. While most Maronites are, in fact residing in Lebanon, many can also be found in Syria, Jordan and the island of Cyprus. For our purposes, however, the Maronites being referred to in this article are those who consider themselves Lebanese and identify with that country's past.

137

Because of the rather limited economic and work opportunities in their own village or coastal town, many adventutous young men driven by their ambition, either decided on their own to leave their country and head toward more promising places, or were sent by their families. In that case, members of a large functionally extended family used to finance the migration overseas of one of their most promising young adults and at the same time promise to take care of his wife and children if he had any. In return, the migrant himself retained some way of communication with his relatives and occasionally sent home some money for land investments or the economic betterment of his kin (Farsoun, 1970:257-271). Coming from an agricultural, traditional background, both types of migrants were expected to be always concerned with the good name, reputation, pride and prestige of their family. Accordingly and despite the distance separating them, the new migrants were supposed to consult the older members of their family group in regard to their religious affiliation and any marital or occupational problems they are faced with in the new country. In conclusion, family loyalty and devotion to the ancestral religion were to remain two of the major forces affecting the life of the migrant in the far-away land.

Antonious-al-Bishallany, landing in Boston in 1854, was reported to be the first migrant to enter the United States from Mt Lebanon starting a movement which developed into a mass one in the early nineties (Hitti. 1967:474). The majority of the new migrants had their first experience with America when they disambarked at New York, Boston or Philadelphia. Many stayed there while others, more ambitious or adventurous, expanded beyond these cities. Being mainly uneducated or unskilled, and handicapped by their inability to use the English language, these early migrants had to resort to peddling, thus travelling first to nearby communities and later across the country.

Studies concentrating on the early life of Arab migrants reported many hoped at first to return to their own village in the shortest time as they left their holdings in family trust. However, becoming more adjusted in time, and thus determined to stay in the new country for a longer period, the majority began to send for their wives, children, parents or whatever family they had waiting for them (Hitti. 1967:58). Moreover, realizing that women and children could be an asset rather than a liability in the United States, they organized the entire family, directing every one's efforts toward reaching a higher social and economic status. Accordingly, while the migrant peddled food, notions, clothes or curios from the Middle-East, his wife often baked and sold bread or sewed dresses at home. Finally, the children were also sent out to sell papers or peddle other items at a very early age (Hitti. 1967:71). Peddling was however considered a temporary occupation as the migrant and his family invested in a private enterprise in the city of their choice as soon as they were able to save some money.

The present paper will examine the patterns of migration, early life in the United States and the extent of integration of one of the largest Maronite communities in an urban settlement. In conclusion, some tentative hypothesis about the community will be also formulated.

Methodology

The present data are derived from a research study conducted in Detroit in 1970. The main objective at that time was the intensive study of a sample of fifty Maronite respondents and their families randomly selected from a list of active Maronite church members all supporting the church and another list of Lebanese migrants provided by the Lebanese Consulate in Detroit. First and second generation respondents were larger in number than the third generation as most of the members of this group are still under eighteen years of age.

At this point, it is important to note that first generation Maronite migrants were defined as members of the community who were born in Lebanon and migrated to the United States after they reached maturity. They were usually described as strongly attached to the ancestral social system and it derivations. The children of these migrants, or migrants who arrived before the age of twelve, reared and schooled in the United States and who know nothing or rarely remember anything about the ancestral society except as it is partially represented in the activities of the members of the ethnic group, constituted the second generation of respondents. Finally, the third generation was composed of their children (Srole and Warner. 1960:29-30).

The main objective of the research was to collect and analyse data about the patterns of migration, the range of behavior and interaction patterns of the randomly selected Maronite respondents while using a standardized questionaire made up of unstructured questions and interviewing each respondent and the present members of his family. The questions were mainly used to collect information on the socio-economic background of the members of the group, the relationship between the migrants and their primary group, the extent of their religious participation in the Maronite church and finally the degree of their identification with the ethnic community which the Maronite church identifies, and the American society in general.

One year later, twenty other members of the Maronite community, all first generation members, were also contacted. Interviewing at that time was mainly unstructured and the respondents were questioned further about the history of the community and their subjective impression regarding the Maronite community as it was when they were young, what changes have occured and finally about their predictions regarding the future of their community. (Ahdab-Yehia. 1970: Chapt. I).

Findings

The first Maronite migrant arrived to Detroit around 1890. Although no one was able to recall his name, it was reported that he settled on Congress street, an area located East of what is presently known as Downtown Detroit, and where some other Arabs, mainly Syrians were already in the grocery business. As he had managed to save some money, he invested in a small food store. His quick success opened the door for a migratory movement to Detroit which developed into a mass one in the early nineties, especially between 1900 and 1925.

Coming from various sections of modern Lebanon, mainly from coastal towns and small villages like Serhel, Hasroun, Tourza, Batroun, Zahle, Kobayat, Beshari, Djeij, Zgorta and finally from Beirut and Tripoli, these early migrants did not settle directly in Detroit but went rather to Southern states like Alabama and Texas in the United States and to Mexico, where some of their relatives were already living. Yet, either unsatisfied with the existing living conditions there, or motivated by an adventurous spirit, they moved gradually to the American northern states, working on their way as farm laborers or peddlers.

Thus, according to one of the main informant of this research study, M. Solomon, a 75 year old migrant who arrived in Detroit in 1911 with twenty other Maronites from Serhel, most of the Maronites who decided to leave Lebanon in search for better economic opportunities were originally heading to Mexico City, South America or Alabama where their other countrymen had already migrated. However, hearing on the boat about the job opportunities in the American northern states, about "the gold that one can find on the streets", and about the success of their compatriots there, some of them changed their path and ended up in different northern cities such as Buffalo, Cincinnati, Detroit, or just staying in New York, Boston or Philadelphia. The rest went to the South where a few Maronites were already in the trade business. While the majority of this latter group is still in Texas or Alabama, some members of the community also migrated to the North, attracted by the business opportunities of the area.

Most of the early Maronite migrants who arrived to Detroit toward the beginning of the twentieth century settled on Congress street and the area around such as St. Orleans Street, Larned, Fort Street, Franklin, La Belle, Sherman, Multett, Jefferson Street and also Dubois and Rispalla in Hamtrack. The successful members of the community acted as middlemen trying to find jobs for the less successful immigrants or the newly arrived ones, renting them rooms in a few apartments they owned. As these individuals became in time more self sufficient and managed to save more money, they invested in small grocery stores, restaurants or in the trading business. They also acted as sponsors to some cousins and close relatives who came to help operate the expanding business. In turn, these individual members sent for their families and either opened their own grocery stores, invested in the restaurant business or went to work at the Detroit Auto plants.

According to M. Solomon and some other first generation informants, a spirit of cooperation was the main characteristic of the Detroit Maronite community at that time. Thus, the already successful members, mainly grocery shops owners dealing with Syrian-Lebanese wholesalers in New York, were as helpful as possible to the newly arrived migrants trying to find jobs for them and harboring them in their own houses until the time they could afford to rent rooms on their own. Some men like Nicholas Nahra, Anthony Peter, John Doueihe are still well remembered for all the help they offered their compatriots. Thus, they not only sheltered them in their houses but also provided them with goods they could peddle from house to house or outside of Detroit, from farm to farm.

Later, when the Detroit auto plants started to attract the majority of migrants because of their relatively high hourly salary, most of the newly arrived Maronites went to work on the assembly plan, some stayed there until their retirement while others were just using this type of job as a means to save money and thus be able to invest in some private business.

As each family increased in number and became prosperous financially, the majority of the members of the community started to invest in the land business. They bought parcels of land in Grosse Point or on the East side of Detroit, and following the example of the middle class Detroiter began to move to this area. By 1920-1925, the community in an exodus to the suburbs and moving away from the inner city and lower class black neighborhoods, gradually spread to Lafayette and the east side of Detroit. This move seems to have been mostly accomplished through a corridor shaped line that linked Congress Street with the east side, mainly Jefferson, Grosse Point and further to St. Clair Shores and Roseville, this depending on the financial situation or the degree of the migrant's ambition or fear from the inner-city problems.

As the Maronite newcomers were very religious, they used at first to go on Sundays to the nearest Catholic church, Sts. Peter and Paul, located on 628 E. Jefferson avenue. When the community increased substantially in size, its members wrote the Maronite Patriarchate in Lebanon, asking for the right to build a Maronite church in Detroit. In answer to their request, Joseph Shabaia who had already organized and built several churches throughout the United States arrived to Detroit in 1915. A church was built on 1555 E. Congress in 1916 and Mass was said according to the Maronite rite for the first time in the newly built St. Maron Church on the 30th of April 1916.

Shabaia was succeeded by Elias P. Asmar as the first appointed pastor of St. Maron church on January 6, 1916. He continued in this capacity until his death in 1933. During this time, St.Maron's school and Sisters' convent were also built in 1921. The school operated from 1921 to June 1934, under the direction of the Sisters of St. Joseph of Nazareth, Michigan, and was closed afterwards because of financial problems. In 1942, some plans were considered for the re-opening of the school but were not successful.

After Elias Asmar's death, Peter S. Sfeir directed the parish until 1937 when he was succeeded by Michael Abdoo who remained Pastor of the Church until his death in 1971. As the community grew larger in size and more influential through the years, the seat of the Exarchate of the Maronite rite in the United States was established in Detroit in 1966. Proud of this honor bequested on their community, the members of this religious group felt the need for a bigger and better place of worship. Accordingly, the old church was replaced by a new one on Kercheval street near downtown and which was dedicated in June 1966.

Recently, the Exarchate was raised to the full rank of diocese by Pope Paul and Bishop Francis Zayek received his staff as first Bishop of the new Maronite Diocese in America on the beginning of June 1972. At this point, it is important to note that the directives explicitly stated that Maronites and all other Eastern Catholic groups have the right to govern themselves according to their own disciplines without interference from the clerics of any other rite. The new diocese includes 150,000 people in 43 parishes in the country while the Detroit parish itself includes about 20,000 members (Ahdab-Yehia. 1970:chapt 2).

Bearing in mind the above information, the second part of this article will focus upon the analysis of some of the present characteristics of the Maronite community in Detroit. The present socioeconomic background of the members of the community will be first examined while the amount of change in the cultural patterns of the respondents will also be studied.

The majority of the respondents reside in the East side of Detroit. Eighty-eight percent are concentrated in the Grosse Pointe area,

Harper Woods and St. Clair Shores, while only twelve percent are living in Birmingham or the northwest side of Detroit. Most families on the other hand, own their houses and have no plans to move. Those who do can generally be found among the respondents who become socially mobile, and because of their higher status plan to reside in better neighborhoods or suburbs.

The occupational pattern of the Maronite respondents seem to gradually differ from their fathers' as 52% of the interviewed people were self-employed:

OCCUPATION OF THE RESPONDENTS AND THEIR FATHERS   (Ahdab-Yehia. 1970: 73)

Occupation	Respondents	%	Fathers	%
Professionals	15	30%	1	2%
Managers and Owners of Medium Business	6	12%	0	0%
Sales, Real Estate, Insurance	4	8%	5	10%
Proprietors	11	22%	22	44%
Skilled, Technical, Clerical	9	18%	2	4%
Manual	5	10%	20	40%
	50	100%	50	100%
Self-Employed	26	52%	40	80%

It appears at this point that the second and third generation Maronite migrants are moving rapidly into professional enterprises requiring special skills and aptitudes. Accordingly, the educational level of the respondents can be judged as average as 98% have some kind of formal education and 40% have been through college:

EDUCATIONAL ATTAINMENT OF RESPONDENTS (Ahdab-Yehia. 1970: 74)

Level of Education	Males	Females	Total	%
No formal Education	0	1	1	2%
Primary School	2	5	7	14%
High and Vocational School	9	13	22	44%
College	10	4	14	28%
Graduate School	5	1	6	12%
	26	24	50	100%

Arabic surnames appear to be rare as the members of the community have always preferred European, especially French surnames, even in their country of origin. It would be interesting to note that 85% of the respondents have changed their Arabic sounding names to American ones, either by changing their spelling or translating them (thus Najib becomes James, Boutros: Peter, Suleiman: Solomon), or by taking an entirely new name like Jones, John or other American names or surnames. On the other hand, the Arabic language itself seems to be losing its popularity. Among the Maronite respondents, only 20% spoke Arabic at home while 60% preferred to speak only English and 20% tended to use both languages:

LANGUAGE SPOKEN AT HOME
(Ahdab-Yehia.   1970: 75)

	Arabic		Both		English	
	M	F	M	F	M	F
First Generation	2	7	3	2	3	3
Second Generation	1	1	2	1	10	8
Third Generation	0	0	1	0	4	2
	3	8	6	3	17	13
	11		9		30	
	22%		18%		60%	

Food customs seem to be surviving more strongly than the language. However, even there, many younger housewives mentioned that they preferred to cook American food during the week as it is easier to prepare. They tended to reserve the typical Lebanese dishes for week-ends or big occasions.

As for the amount of change within the primary group, it appears that the majority of the Maronite respondents are still affiliated to St. Maron and contribute their share for the upkeeping of the Church. Furthermore, the respondents seem to be relatively religious as most of them attend Mass on Sundays. However, as the Maronite rite does not compel the members of the community to go necessarily to a Maronite Church, except when the sacraments are involved, many Maronites prefer the convenience and liturgy of the more numerous Latin churches. This is especially true for those families who have become institutionally involved with the Latin Catholic parochial schools.

Only 38% of the interviewed Maronite families attend Mass at St Maron every week. Among the 48% who go from five to six times a year some declared that they did not like the location of the church near downtown. Others mentioned the fact that as long as their children were in parochial schools, which they also support, they preferred to go to these churches. Moreover, in spite of the increased social activities sponsored by the Maronite Church and the number of clubs and organizations available to general membership, such as the Youth Club, the Ladies' Guild, the Fathers' Club, the Syrian and Lebanese Children of Charity, the Landscape Club, and despite the active influence of two relatively young priests, only 42% of the group attend regularly the social activities of their church or are members of any club. Eighteen percent go from time to time or only on big occasions. Among these, some declared that they attend special activities in order to meet the new members of the community.

Most respondents gave conflicting results when asked whether they thought that the Maronite Church membership had increased or decreased during the past twenty years. Thus 62% thought membership had decreased mainly because of the location of the Church, near downtown and its lower economic surroundings, and disenchantment with some of the formalities of the liturgy, while 38% believed membership had increased because of the efforts of newly appointed young priests, the Bishop residence in Detroit, and finally, because of the efforts of some young Maronites who are trying to coordinate their plans with the priests' in order to attract the members of the community back to St. Maron. On the other hand, the Parish Council which advises the priests on policy changes, the priests and some influential members of the community, aware of the increasing problem of the location of the Church are considering a possible sale and thus a move to Grosse Pointe or St. Clair Shores.

If it is somewhat easy to notice the extent of change in the religious patterns of the Maronite community, it is rather difficult to single out any important change in the attitude of the Maronite respondents toward members of their immediate family.

The family structure of the Maronite respondents still revolves around a highly endogamous marital pattern and divorces are very rare. Eighty one percent of the group are married to Maronites while only five members have latin-rite spouses and five percent have non-Catholic (Protestant and Jewish) spouses. The Catholic marriages were primarily with American members of other nationality groups such as Italians, Irish and Polish. It is interesting that, with the exception of one marriage with a Chaldean, there have been, in this sample, no intermarriages with other Eastern rite Catholic groups or to members of the Greek Orthodox faith, although members of these communities live in the Detroit area.

Distribution of Marriage According to Religion
of Spouse (Ahdab-Yehia: 1970: 67)

	Maronite		Catholic		Protestant		Jewish		Total
	F	M	F	M	F	M	F	M	26
Married	10	9	1	4	0	1	0	1	26
Widowed	4	7	0	0	0	0	0	0	11
Divorced	0	0	0	0	0	0	0	0	0
	14	16	1	4	0	1	0	1	37
	81%				19%				

Furthermore, while 74% of the interviewed follow the traditional American nuclear family household pattern, of the rest only a sizeable minority live with relatives.

The nuclear family itself appears to be run by the father who still represents authority and asks for respect. Thus the majority of the respondents (72%), declared that husbands or fathers are usually the figure of authority in the house. Moreover, when the respondents were asked to give their opinion as to whether children should always obey their parents and thus have an absolute respect for authority, 60% mentioned that they should, while 40% stated that this would vary according to the maturity of the child. Furthermore, all the respondents seemed to think that children should take care of their parents when these would become too old to take care of themselves, even if this meant taking them in their own houses. These results seemed to be consistent with some other reactions as 98% of the sample also mentioned that children should feel love and gratitude toward their parents and thus help them as much as they can in return. While it is possible that the respondents were trying to hide the facts by telling the interviewer what they thought she would want to hear, their replies could be validated to a certain extent as a large number of the first generation members at least had their parents living with them. Moreover, this could be argued as the second and third generation members could be sending their invalid parents to nursing homes, one Maronite member of the community owning such a place.

The marital patterns within the community are still mostly endogamous as almost all the members interviewed were married to Maronites. One member of the second generation respondents even went to his parents' village Serhel in order to choose a bride among his distant relatives. He married his cousin and came back with her. On the other hand, only two respondents were found to have married Protestant or Jewish wives. At this point, it would be also interesting to mention that these spouses did convert to the Catholic faith and have adopted the Maronite rite at least six months before their marriage. The Maronite respondents seemed to have accepted these newcomers as members of the group, however, some of the older people designated them to the interviewer as "the Protestant" or "the Jewish girl", thus indicating their reluctance to include outsiders in the community.

At this point the attitude of the respondents toward an exogamous marriage could be well traced, as many respondents are still opposed to these marriages, especially when the spouse is Moslem or Jewish. Accordingly, the whole community seems to prefer marriages within the group thus thinking that people with the same origins and religious beliefs can understand each other much better. If this is impossible, they tend to settle for at least an interfaith marriage, mainly with American Catholics. This pattern seems to be different for the third generation respondents who are almost indifferent to the ethnic background of their spouses.

Social activities appear to be essential in the life of the Maronite community. Thus, when asked about their visiting patterns, a large number of the respondents mentioned that they visit their friends and close relatives at least once a month if not once a week. Contrary to what one would assume, 72% of the respondents were not related to their friends, and only 28% were confining their visits to members of their family. This seems, however, to be a fairly recent development as first generation respondents visit more relatives than any second or third generation members of the interviewed group.

As the majority of the Maronites are concentrated in an area located on the east side of Detroit, with sometimes four to five residential houses in the same neighborhood, or even on the same block, one would also expect them to have more Maronite friends than American ones. In fact, only 52% of the respondents follow that pattern. This also tends to vary by generation as the younger members of the group interact with more Americans.

These two findings, mainly that one could easily notice a slight change in the visiting and friendship patterns of the younger members of the Maronite community, could be explained by the assumption that as people tend to be more socially mobile, they become less dependent on their family for job placement or inheritance of working patterns and more dependent on outside groups for economic and at the same time social activities.

On the other hand, when asked about their formal association within the community, the majority of the respondents, except for the younger ones, declared that they have belonged, at least for a short period of time, to a Maronite formal organization such as the Junior Hasroun Club, the Immaculate Conception Society of St. Maron Church, St. Michael Society of Serhail, St. Laba's Ladies Society of Hasroun, St. Maron Sacred Heart of Jesus Society, St. George Charity Society, Tourza Brotherhood Society, Zahle American League, Alislaah Kobayat Society, The United North Lebanon Society of America, to mention but a few. At first, these organizations seemed to have attracted a large number of Maronites, especially migrants from the same village or small town. However, they have gradually lost their popularity mainly because of a dissatisfaction with the way they were run. Many respondents described them as a place where members think only about gossiping or fighting with each other and never do constructive work such as trying to interest younger members in their activities or communicate with other Americans of Arab cultural-descent. At this point, a recent tendency is beginning to appear in the community as more members are starting to belong to larger organizations such as the American Lebanese Association and the Arab-American University Graduates, two fairly recent organizations which are trying to incorporate Americans of Arab origin.

Finally, among the interviewed respondents, only 40% tended to identify themselves as Lebanese while others stated that they consider themselves as Americans of Lebanese descent or only Americans. These results seemed to be fairly consistent with those obtained when the respondents were asked about the feelings of the Detroit larger community toward their origins. Thus, 52% declared that Americans tend to consider them as Americans of Lebanese descent while 38% assumed that other Detroit communities know them as Lebanese and only 2% as Arabs:

WHAT RESPONDENTS CONSIDER THEMSELVES
(Ahdab-Yehia. 1970: 106)

	American M	American F	Lebanese M	Lebanese F	Am/Leb M	Am/Leb F	Arab M	Arab F
First Generation	0	0	3	10	4	2	1	0
Second Generation	0	2	3	3	10	5	0	0
Third Generation	0	1	0	0	5	1	0	0
	0	3	6	13	19	8	1	0
	3		19		27		1	
	6%		38%		54%		2%	

HOW RESPONDENTS FEEL AMERICANS CONSIDER THEM
(Ahdab-Yehia. Ibid)

	American M	American F	Lebanese M	Lebanese F	Am/Leb M	Am/Leb F	Arab M	Arab F
First Generation	0	0	5	9	2	3	1	0
Second Generation	3	1	2	2	8	7	0	0
Third Generation	0	1	0	0	5	1	0	0
	3	2	7	11	15	11	1	0
	5		18		26		1	
	10%		36%		52%		2%	

As to the extent to which the respondents use some of the commercial or service organizations of the community, it appeared that 74% listened regularly to the Lebanese radio program which has been operating for 25 years. While the majority also attended almost all the fund raising affairs, church festivals, bake sales and banquets, most of the third generation respondents mentioned that they come very rarely to such occasions.

Thus, it appears that while the members of the Maronite grouping have retained some of their primary family patterns such as endogamous marriages and family structure, the more visible aspects of their cultural background are experiencing a slow but gradual change. Accordingly, if the first generation members still practice some of the customs of their country of origin, the majority of the members of the second and especially third generation are adopting some of the patterns of their new home, such as moving to the suburbs, owning their own homes, working mostly in organizations or bureaucratic structures and speaking only the language of the receiving society.

On the other hand, while one cannot determine the degree and extent of any future change in the religious affiliation of the Maronite members, it can be predicted to a certain extent that the Maronite church will continue to attract newly arrived migrants or older first and second generation members of the community. Accordingly, while retaining most of the religious patterns of their community, such as going to church every Sunday, observing religious norms and attending some of the religious activities of the Maronite Church, the remaining members of the community are starting to attend Roman Catholic Church services. This fact seems to be consistent with an increasingly popular hypothesis, mainly that most ethnic religious groups are identifying progressively with the Roman Catholic socio-religious group rather than their own (Lenski, 1963:362-363). However, if one goes further, it appears that some younger members are becoming active in the church. This new interest has been introduced by some young leaders within the community who are trying to change the traditional Maronite Church in such a way that more Maronite members could become involved.

The Maronite family itself has appeared throughout the study as a fairly close unit where the members still hold most of the values of their immigrant fathers. However, it also appears that some of the problems of the modern American family are beginning to present themselves to the Maronite family as almost all the respondents declared that the demand for freedom on the part of the children is bound to conflict with the desire of the parents to retain control. Furthermore, the majority also stated that the chief areas of dispute between parents and children are mainly caused by a lack of communication and understanding between the two generations. Thus if the solidarity of the family seems to remain almost intact, some members of the third generation are beginning to rebel against parental authority and parents' somewhat rigid manners. This trend appears mainly in the younger generation as individuality and demand for freedom begin to find their way in the Maronite family.

Finally, it appears that the Maronite social organizations are far from providing the community with enough activities that would keep the members' social interaction within the group itself. Because of this lack of "institutional completeness" (Breton, 1964:193-194), at least where the formal associations are concerned, the members of this ethnic religious group are gradually interacting with more Americans than Lebanese Maronites. This is especially true of the American born generation who seem to have more American friends than Maronites, Lebanese or other Arabs.

BIBLIOGRAPHY

Ahdab-Yehia, May
    1970   *The Detroit Maronite Community*. Unpublished Masters Thesis. Wayne State University.

Breton, Raymond
    1964   "Institutional Completeness of Ethnic Communities and the Personal Relations of Immigrants," *American Journal of Sociology*, 70:193-194.

Farsoun, Samih K.
    1970   "Family Structure and Society in Modern Lebanon," in *Peoples and Cultures of the Middle East*, Louise Sweet, editor. New York: The Natural History Press.

Hitti, Phillip K.
    1967   *Lebanon in History*. London: MacMillan.

Lenski, Gerhard
    1963   *The Religious Factor*. New York: Doubleday and Co.

Salibi, Kamal S.
   1962   *The Modern History of Lebanon*. London: Weidenfeld and Micolson.

Maloof, Louis
   1962   *Intact and Immaculate*. Atlanta: St. Joseph Maronite Church Press.

Suleiman, Michael
   1967   *Political Parties in Lebanon*. Ithaca: Cornell University Press.

Srole, Leo and W. Lloyd Warner
   1960   *The Social Systems of American Ethnic Groups*, New Haven: Yale University Press.

An Arab Muslim Community in Michigan

LAUREL D. WIGLE

INTRODUCTION

There are approximately 70,000 Arabic-speaking people and their descendents within the Detroit area. Out of this number, 7,-000 are Moslems. Most Moslems inhabit a section of Dearborn known as the Southend (Elkholy 1966:27, Aswad, this volume). This community is composed primarily of Palestinian, Lebanese and Yemeni Moslems.

Upon entry into the Southend, an observer is immediately struck by its isolation from the rest of Dearborn and Detroit. It is surrounded on three sides by large factories, and on the forth side it is enclosed by a park. Concentration within this area is due to a number of factors, one of which is the prevailing occupational pattern of the Arabs. A great majority of them are employed as laborers within the auto factory. Their occupation as unskilled or semi-skilled laborers does not require advanced training. In fact, many of them do not even find it necessary to learn English.

The Arab community is not only a physical but also a cultural niche. Many traditional Middle Eastern customs are maintained. Along Dix, the main street which bisects the community, the Arabic atmosphere is marked. Numerous coffeehouses are interspersed with Syrian restaurants and grocery stores which import much of their food from the old country. Females are rarely seen on Dix; it is

155

a congregating place for males. Advertisements are written in Arabic and Arabic is the main language spoken on the streets.

Looking at the organization and process of social life within this Arab community and attempting to discover whether or not, or to what extent, new information from surrounding social systems results in cultural change, it is necessary to refer, as Barth (1966:2) suggests, to aspects which govern and affect activity, various features that restrict and canalize the possible course of events. Therefore, attention will be directed towards the necessary or essential variables which govern the course of events. It is a hypothesis of this study that four interrelated features within the Southend determine this process. They are: kinship, religion, community, and nationality.

It is further suggested that patterns of social forms surrounding these four variables.

> "can be explained if we assume that they are cumulative results of a number of separate choices and decisions made by people acting vis-a-vis one another." (Barth 1966:2).

Thus, patterns are arrived at through various processes of interaction and the form they take is an indication of certain restrictions and incentives by which individuals operate. It is through these various instances of interaction that information is passed, sorted out, agreed upon and certain patterns emerge. This information also includes accumulative knowledge and values from the past. This postulate will be discussed with regard to our variables, the first of which is kinship.

KINSHIP

Frequently, discussions of family types within urban areas arrive at the conclusion that the nuclear family is the predominant form. However, in the Southend, kinship ties are not breaking down to the nuclear level. Rather the extended family is a functional reality.

In the rural villages of the Middle East, from which most of the Arabs in the Southend originate, the extended family was a self-contained, self-sufficient unit, controlled by parental authority. Agriculture was the main occupation and the extended family frequently acted as an economic unit. Descent was traced through the male line and the father acted as patriarch of the household. That household was composed of a man, his wife (wives), their unmarried children, and their married children with their partners and offsprings.

A number of changes have occurred within the Southend from this pattern of the rural extended family. Agriculture has been replaced by factory labor and in this respect the family cannot operate as a corporate labor force. Descent is still traced through the male line, however the father's position as the patriarch has been altered. Finally, it is rare to find an extended family operating as a residential unit.

Transformation from agricultural labor to factory labor is a dramatic change for the immigrants. It is not unusual within the Middle East to find factories and commercial firms in large cities employing a number of individuals from the same family. Consequently, some businesses take on an image of an extended family enterprise while other larger firms present facts attesting to numerous extended families being employed within their structure (Abu-Lughod 1967:395; Farsoun 1970:265). However, this is not the case in the large factories found within the city of Detroit. Family connections carry little weight in obtaining a job on an assembly line.

However, while jobs are not always secured through kinship in the Southend, newly arrived immigrants rely on their kindred, who are established within the community, to guide them and direct them to their first job. Out of the first generation males who were interviewed, 80% replied that kinship ties were used for initial contact in the working situation. There is an importance attached to the extended family acting as an "employment agency" in directing and assisting their relatives in finding positions.

It might also be argued that the persistence of strong kinship ties is advantageous in the adaptation of new technological and organizational skills (Weingrod 1970:138). While family members do not work together, they do in fact lend assistance to new immigrants in explaining Western practices associated with factory labor and facilitate the transition to new types of situations. This function is essential if one considers the language barrier faced by an immigrant upon entry into a working situation.

The degree of interaction with other individuals in an urban working situation has also been postulated to result in the break-down of traditional family patterns of immigrants. However, I feel that it is necessary to emphasize the nature of labor found within the Ford factory. Work on an assembly line, I would argue, is more conducive to human and perhaps ethnic isolation.[1] While there is bound to be a certain degree of interaction between the Arabs and members of other cultural systems within the factory, this interaction may be superficial and not have any significant affect on the determining nature of our four variables and their collective significance in generating social patterns in the Arab community.

Farsoun (1970: 257-308) and Williams and Williams (1965:63) have stated that further indications of the relationship between kin-ship and economic factors is illustrated in patterns of immigration. Immigrants working in large cities like Dearborn, frequently send money back to their kin in the country of origin. The well being of many villages is dependent upon the flow of this cash.

The general pattern followed in emigration is the financing of a son's trip by his parents. While this may appear to be a nuclear af-fair, emigration would not be possible without the support of kin in the country of destination. Similarly, the emigrant depends upon his kin to handle his affairs while he is gone.

Within the Southend, families sponsor their relatives and assume responsibility for them. Out of the first generation Arabs inter-viewed, 90% stated that they had some form of kinship ties with residents of the Southend prior to their arrival in this country.

While families occupying the same residence is not prevalent, it is common to find members of an extended family living in close proximity. All of the families interviewed had some members of their extended family living within the Southend, while 40% of them had relatives on the same street. A striking pattern to an out-sider, was the prevalence of the extended family members visiting one another and the extent to which leisure-time was spent together. Especially on weekends, there was a continual flow of in-dividuals and their families in and out of the house of their parents, frequently stopping to eat or drink coffee.

Previously, we noted the importance of kinship in finding jobs. However, it is not limited to this for it is also used in attempts to es-tablish political influence within the city. As a relatively small and non-influential cultural group, members of the Arab community have difficulty in securing their aims when associating with politically powerful outsiders. Therefore, when attempting to obtain desired goals interaction is directed to powerful groups operating within the Arab's own cultural system.

The relationship between kin and the political structure of Dearborn can be understood through the position of the Za'im. Traditionally within the Middle East, the Za'im was a member of the landed elite who acted as an intermediary to the governmental bureaucracy on behalf of his tenants. Operating for the benefit of the Southend, there is one individual who can be classified as a Za'im. This individual appears to be linked with many traditional aspects of Middle Eastern Za'imship. He was a large land owner in southern Lebanon. Within Wayne County he occupies a strategic governmental office and is sometimes in a position to act on behalf of his clients. While he does not reside in the Southend, he has relatives living there and his actual contact with the community is carried out by members of his extended family.

The interrelationship between the father and the family members exhibits some differences from the "typical" Middle Eastern pattern. While the male possesses very definite rights, certain factors militate against his unbridled supremacy. In the first place, there has been a significant change in respect to the bride-price, now referred to as pledge. Sons are no longer dependent upon their fathers to provide them with a pledge; they are capable of earning this money on their own accord. In fact, the pledge is relatively low and it appears to have taken on more of a ritualistic nature. The second factor holding down imperative authority, is that the female is in a potentially more secure economic position in this country. She is not only capable of obtaining a job but also of receiving a higher education.

Thus, we see that the extended family within the Southend is of a new type than that which is found within the Middle East. It is no longer a peasant enterprise. However, it still has significant economic and social functions. Similarly, there have been some changes in the structural relationships within the family. The most important of these changes appears to be associated with the position of the father as an absolute economic controller of the household.

So far in looking at the patterns of social interaction, we have attempted to point out the flow and counter flow of valued goods and services that dictates the relationships. Members of these kinship groups assure themselves a greater value obtained from possessing and maintaining these strong kinship ties than they would obtain if they abandoned such relationships. Specifically, as we have seen from the technological characteristics of Detroit, as they are viewed by the Arabic speaking immigrants, and the continuing relationships of the Arabs with the country of origin, these factors affect the strategy of individuals towards one another and towards members of other cultural systems and there is a tendency to reinforce kinship ties. In contrast to this strict economic transaction, the social interrelationships between members of the extended family and the continuation of its functional structure offers social and psychological rewards, not only to recent immigrants but also to second and third generation Arabs.

RELIGION

Directing our attention to the second variable, that of religion, we can note that there are certain features of a religious nature which reinforce familial ties within the Southend. Among these are births, marriages, funerals, and religious holidays which are occasions on which the extended family unite and thereby reinforce their bonds of membership. Similarly, there are weekly classes at the Mosque for the formal instructing of children in religious beliefs. Attendance at the Mosque on Sunday is a family affair.

In attempting to measure degrees of religiosity within the Southend, Elkholy (1966:99-139) devised a number of scales to test religious beliefs, conventions, and knowledge. Within the community he did not observe any significant correlations between religiosity and sex, between religiosity and occupation or between religiosity and socio-economic status. However, he did note a significant correlation between religiosity and generation and between religiosity and education. Specifically, many second generation and higher educated individuals exhibited religious apathy in such factors as maintaining Ramadan, praying five times daily, attending the Mosque on Friday noon, possessing knowledge concerning the Five Islamic Pillars and so on.

However, Elkholy did observe, and this is supported by our data, that there is considerable resistance on the part of the community to a Moslem girl marrying a non-Moslem male. Even if the man converts to Islam, he is not accepted by the Southend. This is not the case for a Moslem male marrying a non-Moslem female. Since Islam permits men to marry non-Moslems, such unions are acceptable in the eyes of the Southend. However, frequently such women tend to convert and it is obligatory for them to raise their children as Moslems.

In contrast to the findings of Elkholy concerning the barrier between Sunni and Shi'ite sects within the Southend, 80% of the families did not make a distinction between Sunni and Shi'ite marriage. They stated that they are all Arabs and the important factor is to marry a Moslem.

Thus, we see that religious changes within the Southend are affecting certain traditional aspects such as fasting and praying. However, other features, specifically those connected with marriage are not changing. Consequently, it is necessary to make a distinction between two aspects of religion as it affects the community. Bearing in mind some degree of interrelationship between the two, we can note that the first distinction is with religion as a system of theological beliefs which provides a rationale to ritual behavior. It is this aspect of religion that we find changing within the Southend. The second aspect of religion is that of a focus for group loyalty. It is in this area of religion that traditions are rigid. As we noted, it is no longer important if a Sunni marries a Shi'ite. What is significant is that they are both Moslems. It is this factor of religion that commands loyalty from the members of the Arab community.

We can note a degree of interrelationship between the variables of religion and kinship. With respect to diachronic factors, it can be pointed out that in Lebanon there is a high correlation between kinship and religion in such areas as politics and economics. While the sectarian representation is not present in the Southend, a strong interrelationship between the extended family and Islam is still present. For as we observed, there are certain religious occasions and holidays which serve to unite the family and that Mosque attendance is a family affair. Similarly, family marriage patterns strictly conform to religious dictates. Indeed, Islam is a focus of family loyalty.

If we are to look at the cultural system within the Southend in terms of social processes, religious features within this system must also be viewed in a dynamic context. We observed certain changes taking place among some of the doctrines of Islam that relate to ritual, especially among the second and third generations. Therefore, in keeping with out interactional model, in terms of a flow and counter flow of values, we can note that

> "not only is this body of doctrine continuously readjusting the equilibrium between its many tenets but also within those entities and between the doctrine as a whole and its social environment . . . new alternative, contradictive, and redundant religious information circulates within the subsystem, with continuous readjustment attempting to minimize dislocation which would impair the continuity of the system." (Clarke 1968:111)

Thus, we find oscillation among certain aspects of Islam within the Southend. Many first generation individuals still keep Ramadan, refrain from alcohol and pork and pray five times a day. However, individuals of second and third generation and those possessing a higher education appear to be accepting new and contradictory information from outside cultural systems relating to this ritual behavior.

However, among the various generations, socio-economic classes and individuals possessing differing levels of education, Islam is still a focus of group loyalty. The reasons for this are complex, however we can offer a few thoughts. First of all, the impact of Islam on an individual is related to our other three variables, kinship, community, and nationality, and each of these factors have a feedback on one another, thereby acting as a reinforcing mechanism. Secondly, religion appears to have taken on a political nature due to recent events in the Middle East. Being a Moslem is synonymous with being an Arab and there is a strong relationship between this fact and sympathies over the Middle East conflict.

COMMUNITY

It is possible to question why the Arabs in Dearborn have

retained many aspects of traditional Middle Eastern culture, especially in terms of family and relioion, when they are residing in the heart of one of the major industrial cities in the United States. As Abu Lughod (1967:388) has pointed out, it is indeed possible for migrants to reside in sections of a large city yet retain basic similarities to village life. It appears that one of the major factors associated with retention of traditional cultural elements, is the nature of the community to which the immigrants gravitate.

Apart from the mere physical features of the community and aspects of religion and kinship previously mentioned, there are certain indications of community identification. Similar to Tannous' (1942:268) findings for an Arab community in the South, the existence of gossip and secondary group relationships within the Southend are an indication of this identity. Residential and business locations of each family are known by other families. Similarly, personal histories and current happenings to individuals are general knowledge possessed by all except the most recent immigrants.

Salina school, located within the Southend, while not possessing any Arab teachers or not being limited to Arab students, exhibits certain features which tend to reinforce community feelings. Apart from educating the Arab children, it also conducts classes several times a week to teach English to immigrants. A number of parents confided that they preferred to send their children to Salina. They stated that the school was not prejudice against Arabs while prejudice is found in surrounding schools.

Within the community there can be found other social institutions which help to maintain certain Middle Eastern cultural features. The most important of these institutions is the coffeehouse. It is within these shops that men conduct their social and frequently business lives. In fact, the coffeehouse resembles a closed club more than a commercial enterprise.

The coffeehouses on Dix are run by subethnic groups living within the Arab community. Specifically, certain coffeeshops cater only to Lebanese, while others serve only Yemeni, Iraqi, and Palestinian. Within the coffeehouses themselves, tables are arranged according to villages.

Within a Christian Syrian community in Chicago, Haddad

(1969:95-97) attributed the disappearance of the coffeehouse to an increasing breakdown of traditional patterns. She also associated their disappearance with a change in the female's status, for women are not permitted within coffeehouses. This may have a certain amount of significance for the Southend. For within the Dearborn community, there is no indication of coffeehouses being replaced by other institutions such as a more Western club found in the Chicago community. And as previously stated, females not only refrain from frequenting the coffeehouses, they are also rarely seen on Dix. This may in fact indicate that there is not a complete alteration of the traditional female role.

Directing our attention to the interrelating aspects found in kinship, religion, and community, we will note that first of all, the Arab community is composed of a number of extended families possessing a common denominator of a distinct religious identity. A number of institutions within the community provide reinforcement of kin and religious values. The Mosque located on Dix instructs children in the teachings of Muhammed and conducts services attended by the families *en masse*. A school is available which not only educates Arab children but also teaches new immigrants English. Coffeehouses can be found all along Dix and their restrictions on clientele reflect the continuation of the traditional separation of males and females.

It is within the boundaries of the community that the Arabs enter into most of their interpersonal relationships. It is in this context that various aspects of associationships are reinforced and certain values become systematized and shared. This systematization, as we have noted, results through a process of interaction in which individuals are confronted with the necessity of evaluating alternatives. The community is an essential variable in this process due to the fact that when attempting to place a value on certain aspects, other people's decisions frequently act as a guide.

NATIONALITY

Directing our attention to nationality, we noted that in the Southend the Arabs are mostly from Lebanese, Palestinian, and Yemeni descent. This distinction is marked. It was pointed out that ethnic groups frequent specific coffeehouses. This also applies to the purchasing of food from various grocery stores. Social and recreational activities apart from being carried out mainly by the extended family, are further limited to ones subethnic group. Even among third generation Arabs, the tendency is still strong to find one's friends in one's subethnic group.

Apart from these ethnic distinctions, there appears to be further stratification along class lines. The main difference is between individuals who were/are the landed elite in the old country and their peasantry. This distinction is found in both social and economic realms. Individuals from the upper classes in the Middle East tend to be involved in more profitable ventures in Detroit. Many of them are store owners, professional educators, members of high bureaucratic offices and so on.

Specifically, a large land owning family from southern Lebanon migrated to the Southend. Members of this family include grocery store owners, a lawyer, a sheriff, a car dealer, an appliance store owner, a religious leader, and a chairman for an electoral district. The elites also maintain certain features which provide them with status in the Middle East and still function within the Southend. For example, sheikhship is inherited and individuals possessing that title are respectfully acknowledged. There is also the persistence of the Za'im.

In contrast to this group, individuals of peasantry background are employed mainly in factory work and occupy a lower social status. However, there is some tendency among second and third generations of this class to seek different employment and aim for higher education.

It may appear from this analysis of nationality that the interactional model used throughout the paper would tend to lose much of its strength in attempting to explain social process in the Southend. For we noted within the community itself there are marked distinctions between ethnic and social groups and interaction among them is somewhat limited.

However, it is in this context that it is necessary to evaluate the larger and more encompassing aspect of nationality, that of being an Arab. This feeling is strong and pervades all subethnic groups. While within community boundaries subethnic distinctions will be observed, when facing the external environmental cultural systems, individuals unite as Arabs in the face of non-Arabs.

Especially in light of the continuing Middle East conflict, many stereotypes being applied to Arabs and the generally unfavorable reports against the Arab world, that the Arabs in the Southend exhibit many features of Pan-Arabism. This is true even among third generation Arabs. For as Elkholy (1966:94) noted, their political orientation towards Arab nationalism is strikingly similar to that of the first generation and they have developed many sympathetic feelings towards the country and culture of their ancestry.

Therefore, we now direct our model of interaction to the transactions that take place between Arabs and non-Arabs. It is in this context that certain values, especially those surrounding Arabism as exemplified by Arab family structure, Arab religious idelogy and Arab community, reinforce one another and become systematized. Through exchanges of information with external cultural systems, certain subsequent choices made by Arabs in the Southend tend to be shared, irrespective of subethnic group, and thereby act as available guides for the behavior of others. And as Barth notes, this leads towards integration and institutionalization of cultural features.

> "In an on-going system, where patterns of behaviour are generated from a set of shared values, the resolution of individual dilemmas of choice by the construction of overarching principles of evaluation will have a feedback effect on the shared values. The shared values will be modified and 'corrected' in the direction of greater consistency and integration and other patterns of choice and will in turn be generated:" (Barth 1966:14-15).

In conclusion it can be stated that in the Southend, there are four main variables which are associated with organization and social process. They are kinship ties, religious orientation, the community itself and Arab nationality. Members of the Southend interact with one another and individuals from other cultural systems. In these interactions, information is transmitted and results in certain cultural changes. However, evaluations are continually made in regards to this new information. The cumulative advantages associated with possessing strong kinship ties, living in the Southend, and possessing Islam and Arabism as a group loyalty are measured against other forms of interaction and relationships, with the former category being attributed preference.

NOTES

[1]Concerning ethnic isolation, numerous Arabs reported that they were not allowed to work on specific equipment, especially that which was destined for Israel.

BIBLIOGRAPHY

Abu-Lughod, Janet
   1967   "Migrant adjustment to City Life: The Egyptian Case," in Potter, J., M. Diaz and G. Foster (eds.) *Peasant Society: A Reader*. Boston: Little, Brown & Company.

Aswad, Barbara C.
   1974   "The Southeast Dearborn Arab Community Struggles for Survival Against Urban "Renewal"". (This volume)

Barth, Fredrik
   1966   *Models of Social Organization*, Royal Anthropological Society Occasional Papers #23. London

Clarke, David
   1968   *Analytical Archaeology*. London: Barnes & Noble Inc.

Elkholy, Abdo
   1966   *Arab Moslems in the United States*. New Haven: College & University Press.

Farsoun, Samih
   1970   "Family Structure in Modern Lebanon," in Sweet, L. (ed) *Peoples and Cultures of the Middle East*, Vol. 11. Garden City: Natural History Press.

Haddad, Sabia
   1969   "The Woman's Role in Socialization of Syrian Americans in Chicago." in Hagopian E.C. and A. Paden (eds.) *The Arab-Americans*. Wilmette: Medina University Press.

Tannous, Afif
   1942   "Acculturation of an Arab-Syrian Community in the Deep South," *American Sociological Review:* Vol. 7

Williams, H.W. and J. Williams
   1965   "The Extended Family as a Vehicle of Culture Change," *Human Organization*, Vol. 24.

Research on Arab Child Bilinguals*

ALEYA ROUCHDY

The literature on bilingualism has been increasing steadily; however the study of Arab-American bilinguals has not been given a fair share by interested linguists and sociolinguists. The writer conducted research in the Detroit metropolitan area that deals with this underdeveloped aspect of bilingual studies. Detroit and its suburbs suburbs are a unique laboratory for studying immigrants and their descendants of Middle Eastern communities. The Arabic speaking people in this community exceeds 70,000 persons. It is the largest Arab community in the U.S. and one of the oldest.

This research is based on the study of twenty-two cases. The total number is not large enough to draw definite conclusions; however the writer hopes that it will stimulate further research studies in this area. Such a study could also be of practical use to educators interested in different clusters of ethnic groups in the U.S. as to the achievement of their young bilingual members in schools.

The Subjects

The subjects under study are mostly first generation Americans between the age of eleven and fourteen. Some were born in an Arab country but came as infants to the United States. They learned Arabic in their homes speaking to their parents. The subjects are all coordinate bilinguals since they have learned their two languages in different contexts. One language is learned at school,

169

English, whereas the other is spoken at home, Arabic. This aspect of learning the two languages contrasts with that of compound bilinguals who learn the different languages in the same situation. Osgood maintains that the coordinate bilingual experiences less interference than the compound bilingual because the former can easily keep the two languages apart (1965:141). Actually the speech of both coordinate and compound bilinguals can have phonological, syntactic and lexical interference, but the main point is that the reactions to interference is different. A compound bilingual can correct or control any interference, especially when faced with a monolingual speaker. A coordinate bilingual may have no other choice than to use his dominant language as reference.

In this research the writer differentiated between two types of bilinguals based on their competence and performance in the languages they speak:[1]

	competence	performance
Speaker A	+	+
Speaker B	+	-

Speaker A is a communicative bilingual or an active bilingual. He can understand and reproduce the first and second languages he speaks, English and Arabic. Speaker B is a latent bilingual who understands the second language Arabic, but has a hard time reproducing it in some situations. These two groups of bilinguals are each in turn divided into naive and sophisticated bilinguals according to the speaker's "facultę de langue." The "facultę de langue" is based on the idea that languages have universal properties "attributable to human mentality." (Chomsky, citing Von Humbolt, 1966:21). Its different degrees separate a naive from a sophisticated monolingual or bilingual speaker. The naive bilingual applies more often particular rules on one language while speaking another language. An example of this would be a Frenchman, living in the United States and considered a perfect bilingual, who might say in English 'I go to the movie for to see an amusing film' based on the perfectly correct French 'je vais au cinema pour voir un film amusant.' The English version is rejected by a native English speaker as being substandard since it is used only in some dialects. Another point of differentiation between naive and sophisticated bilingual speakers is the involuntary construction which the former group is unable to correct when asked. An example supporting the above statement would be the phrase 'the cat on the roof' which has undergone an optional ellipsis, since one could also say 'the cat which is on the roof'. The naive speaker fails to see the similarity between the two structures. The sophisticated bilingual has more awareness of universal and particular rules in languages and although he cannot escape interference he might be able to correct some of the deviation in the languages he speaks.

There are certain factors that affect the degree of bilingualism of the individual such as the place where the languages were learned, the age of learning and the motivation for learning the languages. Due to these factors some bilinguals have better control of the different systems of the languages they speak than other bilingual speakers. Some can shift from one language to the other and discuss different subjects in the different languages; however at a certain time and under a certain situation such adroit bilinguals feel at ease with one specific language, usually the dominant language.

The names of the twenty-two subjects were obtained from the Salina School's counselor in Southeast Dearborn, Michigan. They were chosen on the basis that Arabic was learned in the U.S. Sixteen of them were born in the U.S. and six came as infants. A schedule was arranged between the counselor and the researcher to interview each informant for thirty minutes. First, the field worker filled out a biographical questionnaire dealing with information such as: birthplace, age, sex, if not born in the U.S. the date of arrival, languages spoken at home and finally the parents' level of education. Second, four objective tests, which have been recorded, were given to each subject. The tests are mainly based on the ones suggested by Macnamara (1967:58-77) and which the author used in two previous researches when studying a case of bilingualism (Rouchdy 1971). The tests are:

1. Word Translation Test: designed to measure the subjects' vocabulary in different areas. The words were grouped into different categories: nouns and adjectives. The nouns included words

associated with the house, or related to school or general nouns such as car, tree, street, etc. This test was given in both languages, Arabic and English[2]. (See Table 1.)

2. Sentence Translation Test: where idioms and specific syntactic structures were stressed. This test was also given in both languages[3]. (See Tables 2 and 3.)

3. Reaction Time Test: designed to determine the bilingual capacity in giving as many words as possible in a limited time starting with specific phonemes in both languages, Arabic and English. The subject under study had one minute for each phoneme. This test was used to study the effect of bilingualism on the subjects' performance in producing words in English or Arabic. One of the writer's aims in giving this test was to find out if the emphatic (velarized) and non-emphatic (non-velarized) phonemes of Arabic have merged in the underlying representation of the bilingual speakers.

TABLE 1   WORD TRANSLATION TEST

The table demonstrates the average and standard deviation of percentage of correct translations. The results are based on the translation of ten words given for each group of words.

Group of Words	Part I Average and Standard Deviation of percentage of correct translation Arabic to English		Part II Average and Standard Deviation of percentage of correct translation English to Arabic	
Nouns related to household	80.09	9.28	58.18	25.81
Nouns related to school	48.63	25.07	43.18	23.84
General nouns	77.27	19.15	57.72	25.69
Adjectives	68.63	14.53	51.81	20.56

Table 1 shows that the average percentage of correct words translated from Arabic into English is higher than that from English into Arabic. Thus, the subjects translate better when the message is given to them in Arabic. Since the two parts of the Word Translation Test were given at different times, the same word was sometimes chosen as a message in both Arabic and English. The majority of the subjects were able to translate the word in English when hearing it in Arabic, but not when the situation is reversed. The subjects knew the meaning of the word in both languages but were unable to produce it in Arabic. Based on this test the researcher classified the bilingual subjects as latent bilinguals who had competence in Arabic not reflected in their performance.

Table 1 reflects an interesting aspect and that is the low average of correct translation of words related to school in both languages. The subjects use these words daily at school but do not know their equivalents in Arabic. For instance when the word 'principle' was given as message in English or Arabic, the majority of the subjects were unable to translate it in either Arabic or English.

The results of this test give an indication of the type of conversations held in the subjects' homes.

Table 2 shows that the subjects' lowest performance in translating sentences was when the 'number-agreement' structure was stressed. It is in this part of the test that grammatical rules were mostly violated. The table also indicates the interference occurred, and mostly when 'verbal-prepositions' were translated.

The interference in the subjects' responses was as follows:
1. The translation of English items word for word. The result was a sentence that is Arabic in phonology but English in style. This aspect of interference occurred mostly when verbal prepositions were translated.
2. The modification of the item, so that it will fit the pattern of the recipient language. In this case interference occured in both ways from Arabic to English and from English to Arabic. For instance the bilingual would say 'yidayyit' or 'yibarrak' for the English expressions 'to have a date' or 'to park a car'.
3. The retaining of items without translation, a one way interference from English to Arabic. Words such as 'make up' or 'stove' were frequently used in the middle of Arabic sentences.

In the material collected from the Sentence Translation Test, the researcher did not encounter calques from English in the word order of Arabic sentences. The subject sometimes could not remember the translation of an English word and he would thus use the English item, without disturbing the Arabic pattern. An example would be the translation of the structure 'the smart boy - - -' as /ʔil walad ʔil smart/ where the adjective follows and agrees with the noun it modifies, although 'smart' is a transferred English word.

TABLE 2 SENTENCE TRANSLATION TEST

This table shows the average and standard deviation of the different responses to the different syntactic structures emphasized within the sentences. Translation from English to Arabic.

syntactic structures examined	number of sentences given	grammatical response (1)° Avg	grammatical response (1)° StD	anglicized response (2)° Avg	anglicized response (2)° StD	ungrammatical response (3)° Avg	ungrammatical response (3)° StD	no response (4)° Avg	no response (4)° StD
Placement of negatives	7	5.55	1.93	0.23	0.50	0.68	1.39	0.55	1.44
Number agreement	6	3.86	1.73	0.13	0.48	1.55	1.46	0.41	1.24
Use of correct tense of verbs	13	8.45	3.13	2.64	1.95	0.59	1.71	1.32	2.68
Use of correct verbal position	8	4.66	1.58	2.27	1.39	0.14	0.61	0.95	1.70
Relative clauses	6	4.45	1.88	0.14	0.33	1.36	1.78	0.32	1.23

(1) When none of the grammatical rules have been violated.
(2) When the subjects use English words, or translate them literally in the Arabic sentences, i.e. when interference occurs from English to Arabic.
(3) When grammatical rules are violated.
(4) When there is complete silence.

The researcher chose the syntactic structures, listed in Table 2, from the recorded biographical questionaire and conversation that she had collected. The subjects were more at ease than when the objective tests were offered. They were mixing rules that resulted in syntactic errors mainly due to a certain linguistic laziness. The subjects knew that they shared with the researcher a common factor, bilingualism, which will help her understand them. Haugen referred to this attitude as being the result of "the law of least effort" which led to a poor performance. Therefore the subjects were given the Sentence Translation Test to evaluate, in a way, their level of competence in Arabic. From the results shown on Table 2, it can be said that the bilingual subjects knew the basic transformations in Arabic, thus their earlier performance was not a total manifestation of their competence.

Table 3 (the translation from Arabic into English) shows that the subjects' responses in English were mostly grammatical. The Arabicized responses were sentences where the subject literally translated Arabic idioms into English which resulted in sentences such as 'he opens the TV' for 'he turns on the TV' or 'she closes the light' for 'she turns off the light'.

Table 4 indicates that the bilingual subjects recalled more words in English than in Arabic. If the test was given to monolinguals (Arabs or Americans) the researcher would have been in a better position to examine the effect of bilingualism on the subjects' speed in producing words[4].

During the Reaction Time Test, which measured the quantity rather than the quality of performance, some of the subjects did not differentiate between velarized (emphatic) and non-velarized (non-emphatic) phonemes in Arabic. The word /ḍarb/ and /ṣu:t/ were given as having initial /d/ and /s/ (in such a case they were not computed at all). The researcher was interested in finding out if the Arabic phonemes emphatic/non-emphatic have merged in the subjects' underlying representation. She thus gave each subject a list of English words to translate into Arabic. The Arabic translation of the words on this list had /s/ and / . / or /d/ and / . / occuring initially, medially or finally. Fifty percent of the subjects gave the correct pronounciation, differentiating properly between the emphatic/non-emphatic sounds. Two thirds of the remaining fifty

TABLE 3   SENTENCE TRANSLATION TEST

This table shows the average and standard deviation of the different responses to the different Arabic sentences.
Translation from Arabic to English.

Number of Arabic sentences examined	Grammatical response (1)°		Arabicized sentence (2)°		Ungrammatical sentence (3)°		No response (4)°	
	Avg	StD	Avg	StD	Avg	StD	Avg	StD
Eleven grammatical structures where idioms were stressed	8.31	1.96	1.27	1.24	0.50	0.74	0.90	1.15

(1) When one of the grammatical rules have been violated.
(2) When the subjects use Arabic words, or translate them literally in the English sentence, i.e. that is when interference occurs from Arabic to English.
(3) When grammatical rules are violated.
(4) When there is complete silence.

TABLE 4°   REACTION TIME TEST

This table demonstrates the average and the standard deviation of the number of words, starting with a specific phoneme, produced by 22 students. Time allowed for each phoneme was one minute.

Initial Phonemes Arabic	Average Standard Deviation of the number of Arabic words		Initial Phonemes English	Average Standard Deviation of the number of English words	
	Avg	StD		Avg	StD
/d/	2.82	1.58	/d/	8.32	3.01
/s/	4.05	2.49	/s/	10.14	3.90
/m/	4.05	2.76	/p/	9.27	4.39
/n/	2.68	1.92	/v/	4.86	2.54
/b/	3.50	2.34	/m/	9.22	2.55
/l/	1.68	1.65	/n/	7.09	3.21
/ s /	1.45	2.04	/b/	8.54	4.49
/ḍ /	0.68	0.99	/l/	9.64	3.99

°The phonemes /p/ and /v/ were left out of the column under Arabic phonemes since they do not exist in the Arabid phonological system. Eleven out of the twenty two informants when asked to give Arabic words starting with /p/ or /v/, answered that there was no such sounds in Arabic. The other eleven either remained silent, trying to remember words with /p/ or /v/, or they gave words where /b/ → [p] — [$^{+vl}_{+stop}$] such as /ʔibtasam/ → [ʔiptasam] or /ʔibtasam or /bita:9i/ → [pita:9i]. As for /v/ they responded that there was no such sound in Arabic.

percent confused the two sounds and could not hear the difference when the researcher pronounced it for them. The other one-third remained silent and did not respond to this part of the test. The second fifty percent is thus classified by the researcher as naive bilinguals since they apply particular rules of one language, English while speaking another language, Arabic, and since they were also unable to correct their errors when it was pointed out to them.

Epilogue

The four tests that were given to the subjects did measure their proficiency in the areas of expression and translation. In all of the tests the subjects' average score in English performance is higher than it is in Arabic; however the qualitive and the quantitative evaluations of the bilinguals should also depend on the four factors which were mentioned by Weinreich (1973:69). First, the order of learning. In all of the cases the subjects learned Arabic before

English at home. Second, the mode of use. This includes visual reinforcement and oral use of the language. Among the subjects under study the visual enforcement is stronger in English. Third, the usefulness of communication. English is more useful to the subjects at school and outside their community. Finally, the emotional involvement. The subjects are involved in both languages, English being the language of the country and Arabic being the dominant language of the community[3].

TABLE 5
This table demonstrates the rating of
the language within certain aspects.

Measuring aspects for language dominance	English	Arabic
Relative proficiency	°	+
1. understanding	+	+
2. expression	°	+
Mode of use		
1. visual	°	+
2. oral	+	+
First Training		
Emotional involvement		+
1. friendship	+	+
2. patriotic attachment	°	+
Usefulness in communication	+	+

Note: + indicates positive rating of a language at a certain point.
         ° indicates that the rating of one language is higher.

Following Weinreich's model on language dominance Table 5 shows the rating of the language within certain aspects. Two aspects are equally important to the bilingual subjects in using English or Arabic: the oral mode of use and the usefulness in communication.

Conclusion

The objective of this research was three fold: first, as a linguist the writer is interested in bilingualism for its explanation of language change occuring in the speech of first generation Arab-Americans, that is studying the interference occuring in their Arabic as well as English speech. Based on the results of the four objective tests, one can conclude that interference from English into Arabic is higher than from Arabic into English. Thus bilingualism did affect the subject's performance in Arabic. Second, the writer was not only interested in examining interference that occur in the speech of the bilingual informants, but it was her aim to use the bilingual's performance as data to investigate competence, that is the underlying system of rules that the bilingual knows but does not necessarily use, and to demonstrate that bilingualism belongs to both domain competence and performance. "If we wish to explain performance we must show how it derives from competence . . . " (McNeil, 1966:17). Third, the researcher was also interested in pointing out the socially dominant language in the community and since Arabic is the dominant language, it ought to be part of the school curriculum in this community.

NOTES

*This article is published with permission from Newbury House Publishers from *Problems in Applied Educational Sociolinguistics*, Glenn Gilbert, ed., Newbury House, 1974. The title of the article has been changed from "Elicitation Techniques for Research on Child Bilinguals."

[1]The sign (-) implies a certain knowledge but less than that shown by (+) since any performance implies some competence.

[2]For a description and social analysis of the community, see the articles by Aswad and by Wigle in this volume.

[3]The writer in her previous research (Rouchdy, 1971) differentiated between objective and subjective tests. The objective tests are mechanical tests that require quick responses from the subject. The subjective tests were designed to allow the subject to use his own vocabulary and syntax, such as describing a picture to the examiner.

[4]This test will be conducted in the future by the researcher and the results will be compared with those of the bilingual subjects.

[5]This community consists of two homogenous Arab ethnic groups who migrated to the U.S. during the last few decades and came to live in the area known as the Dix section which is adjacent to the Ford Motors industrial complex (Rouge Plant). At the present time this ethnic community is challenging and fighting through the federal court the decision of the city government of Dearborn to evict them from their homes in order to demolish the physical structure of that community under the pretext of urban renewal. This collective response on the part of the community reflects the strength of their ethnic solidarity which is apparent in their frequent use of the Arabic language as noticed by visitors to the community.

References

Chomsky, Noam
   1966   *Cartesian Linguistics.* New York: Harper & Row.

Macnamara, John
   1967   "The Bilingual's Linguistic Performance: A Psychological
           Overvies," *Journal of Social Issues,* 23, p. 58-77.

McNeil, David
   1966   "Developmental Psycholinguistics," *Genesis of Language: A
           Psycholinguistic Approach,* eds. Frank Smith & George A.
           Miller Cambridge: MIT Press.

Osgood, Charles, and Thomas A. Sebeok, eds.
   1965   *Psycholinguistics: A Survey of Theory and Research Problems.*
           Bloomington: Indiana University Press.

Rouchdy, Aleya
   1971   "A Case of Bilingualism: An Investigation in the Area of
           Lexical & Syntactic Interference in the Performance of a Bilin-
           gual Child," Presented to the Modern Language Association,
           Chicago.

Weinreich, Uriel
   1963   *Languages in Contact: Findings and Problems.* The Hague:
           Mouton.

An Arab-American Bibliography

PHILIP M. KAYAL[*]

Cataloguing research reports, data, texts and general information on Arab Americans is difficult because of the wide range of peoples and nationalities who are Arabic speaking and resident in this country. The fact that Arab Americans are both Christian and Moslem and immigrants over several decades as well as from a host of countries does not simplify the task any. Researchers, however, might be wise to check the following general sources before they refer to the specific items listed at the end.

To begin with, the histories of Moslem Americans are somewhat easier to locate simply because they are less numerous and the majority are of more recent origin. An excellent source, which is complete with bibliography, is Abdo A. Elkholy's *The Arab Moslems In the United States* (New Haven: College & Univer. Press, 1966). Journals and collections like the *Encylopedia Britannica, The Encylopedia of Islam* and *The Moslem World, The Palestine Digest* and the trade magazines of the various oil companies like *ARAMCO World Magazine* often times carry articles on and by Arabs in the diaspora. They also help clarify terms and concepts

[*]This bibliography could not have been completed without the assistance of Dr. Barbara Aswad of Wayne State University and Dr. Steward McHenry of the University of Vermont.

which are unique to the Middle East such as 'millet,' rite, Eastern Churches, Sun'ni Moslem, etc.

Good sources of the communities' activities can also be found in such national tabloids as the *Muslim Star,* published by the Federation of Islamic Associations in the U. S. and Canada (headquarters in Detroit), and the *Bulletin,* published by the Islamic Center in Washington, D. C. Also such newspapers as *The Arab-American Message* and *Al Bayan* (Both published in Detroit) carry news of the various Moslem communities. For historical information, sometimes local libraries will have copies of past suspended newspapers. For example the Detroit Public Library has some copies of some six suspended tabloids in the Detroit region.

The Arab Christian experience is more complicated because it is diffused throughout several areas and originated in so many different nation-states. Because most of the early migrants were in fact Christians, descriptive and educational religious texts written in this country after 1915 often times have reference to Syrian and/or Lebanese Christian Americans. These immigrants were members of Eastern Christianity which is partially Roman Catholic and partially Eastern Orthodox. The Catholic segment is divided into several rites and it is under this rubric, i.e., Eastern Churches or Eastern rites that much material on their religious experiences in this country can be found. For example, *The Eastern Churches Quarterly* and *Diakonia* have several articles on the Maronites of Lebanon in America and the assimilation of American Melkites who are primarily Syrians. The Orthodox experience has been treated in these journals as well as the *St. Vladimir's Seminary Quarterly.* See especially, Constantine Volaitis, "The Orthodox Church in the United States as Viewed from the Social Sciences," *St. Vladimir's Sem. Quart.,* 5:1-2 (1961), pp. 63-87.

Researchers are advised that they must not expect articles on Arab-Americans to be necessarily indexed under that title. The Christian Arab population, for example, is described and analyzed in texts or articles on "national parishes," "Eastern Catholics," or even "Syrian Christians" when in fact the authors usually mean and are describing "Lebanese Catholics." All these categories, therefore, should be searched out thoroughly.

The most important source of histories and biographies of the various Arab communities in this country are found in the *Anniversary Journals* of each independent parish or Mosque as well as those of the larger religious bodies they belong to. For example, each Arab Christian parish has traditionally published a yearly journal depicting its growth, changes and history for its readers. On the national level, it is wise to utilize the Journals of the *Syrian Orthodox Youth Organization* (SOYO), the *Melkite Exarchate* and the *Maronite Eparchy*. One journal, *The Melkite Digest* and a survey text entitled *Melkites In America* (Boston: Melkite Exarchate, 1971) are especially important.

In a similar and related vein are the journals of the local and national Syrian/Lebanese and other Arab social organizations. In particular the journals of the *Haddad Foundation*, the *ALSAC* organization of entertainer Danny Thomas, the publications of the *Association of Arab-American University Graduates* (AAUG), and the *National Federation of Syrian-Lebanese Clubs* as well as their affiliated chapters. More important as preliminary sources are the publications of the *Al-Hoda* press such as *The Syrian World*, (on microfilm at the Library of Congress), *The Syrian Commerce of New York, The Syrian-Business Directory (1908-1909)*, *Al-Hoda* (in Arabic as is *Al-Bayan*), the *Lebanese-American Journal, Heritage*, and *Action* which appears primarily in English and gives contemporary information on all United States Arab communities. The emerging Egyptian community in North America puts out *Misr* an Arab bi-weekly newspaper. It originates in Jersey City, New Jersey. Another new publication is the *Arabic Tribune* published by the Federation of Arab Immigrants, Toledo, Ohio. Most of these tabloids can be located through the services of *Al-Hoda* or *Action* in New York City.

Another available and useful primary source for information on Syrian/Lebanese immigration and subsequent assimilation can be found in the autobiographies of the early Christian pioneers. For example, *I Grew With Them* by Rev. Cyril Anid (Jounieh, Lebanon: Paulist Press, 1967) is actually the assimilation story of the Catholic Syrians of Paterson, New Jersey. Similar texts are Rev. Abraham Rihbany, *A Far Journey* (Boston: Houghton, Mifflin Co., 1914), and Salom Rizk, *Syrian Yankee* (Garden City: Doubleday, 1943). A humorous account of growing up Lebanese in the United

States is found in William P. Blatty's *Which Way to Mecca, Jack?* (New York: B. Geis Assoc., 1960).

Generally speaking, the classic American texts on immigration barely touch on the Arab-Americans who are variously described as Turks, Asians, or Assyrians. Some useful surveys, however, can be found in *One America* (New York: Prentice-Hall, 1952) by Brown and Roucik; *Around the World in New York* (New York: Century Co., 1924) by Konrad Berovici and William J. Cole's *Immigrant Races in Massachusetts* (Boston: Dept. of Education, 1919).

Two other publications deserve special mention here. The Association of Arab-American University Graduates has published a collection of articles entitled *Arab-Americans: Studies in Assimilation* (Wilmette, Illinois: Medina University Press, 1969) and edited by Elaine Hagopian and Ann Paden. Each contribution is separately listed below. A doctoral dissertation by Dr. Adele L. Younis is also noteworthy. Entitled, *The Coming of the Arabic-Speaking People to the United States* it contains a complete bibliography of all material appearing on Arab Americans up to 1961. Newspaper reports are also catalogued. Currently numerous attempts are being made to collect materials on the various communities before they are lost or thrown away. The AAUG has established an Archives Collection for North America in conjunction with the Center for Immigrant Studies of the University of Minnesota in Minneapolis. Some local AAUG chapters, such as that of Detroit, are also collecting materials for a local collection.

In addition, of course, the bibliographies at the end of each article in this book can be consulted by the reader.

Additional References

Abdah, Moshid
    1929   *From the Visions of Life: A Group of Stories and Social Articles* (Arabic). Boston: The Syrian Press.

Abu-Laban, Baha
    1969   "The Arab-Canadian Community," in Hagopian and Padden, *op. cit.*, pp. 18-36.

Addia, William E. & Thomas Arnold
    1964   *Christians of Chaldean Rite, A Catholic Directory*. London: Rutledge & Kegan Paul.

Adeney, Walter F.
  1965   *The Greek and Eastern Churches*. Clifton, New Jersey.
          Reference Book Publishers.

Al-Hoda
  1968   *The Story of Lebanon and Its Emigrants*. New York: Al-Hoda
          Press.

Antebi, Michael
  1960   "The Syrian Sephardim of Bensonhurst," *Jewish Press*, Sept.
          23rd.

Arida, Nasib & Sabri Andrea
  1930   *Directory of Syrian Americans in the United States*. New York:
          Syrian American Printers.

Beynon, E. D.
  1944   "The Near East in Flint, Michigan: Assyrians and Druze and
          Their Antecedents," *Geographical Review*, 24 (January), pp.
          234-274.

Bd. of Directors
  1970   *Golden Jubilee of St. Joseph's Maronite Catholic Church,
          Olean, New York*. Parish Council.

Barclay, Harold
  1961   "A Lebanese (Moslem) Community in Lac LaBiche, Alberta,"
          Immigrant Groups, Jean L. Elliot, ed., Scarborough, Ontario:
          Prentice-Hall of Canada, Ltd.

Bengough, W.
  1895   "The Syrian Colony," *Harpers Weekly*, August 3rd., p. 746.

Berger, Morroe
  1958   "America's Syrian Community," *Commentary*, 25:4 (April),
          pp. 314-323.

  1959   "Americans from the Arab World" in James Kritzeck & R.
          Bayly Winder (eds.) *The World of Islam*. New York. St.
          Martins Press. Pp. 351-372.

Cahnman, Werner
  1944   "Religion and Nationality," *American Journal of Sociology*,
          49:6 (May), pp. 524-529.

Chuaqui, Benedicto
  1952   "Arabs in Chile," *Americas*, 4:12 (Dec.) pp. 17-29.

Davies, R. P.
    1949   "Syrian Arabic Kinship Terms," *Southwestern Journal of Anthropology*, 5:3 (Autumn), pp. 244-252.

Duncan, Norman
    1903   "A People from the East," *Harpers Magazine* (March), pp. 62-65.

Elkholy, Abdo A.
    1969   "The Arab Americans: Nationalism and Traditional Preservations," in Hagopian and Paden, *op. cit.*, pp. 3-17.

Goldberg, Merle
    1969   "Casbah In Brooklyn," *New York Magazine*, July 14th, pp. 62-65.

Grigorieff, Dimitry
    1961   "The Historical Background of Orthodoxy in America,'$ *St. Vladimir's Seminary Quarterly*, 5:1,2. pp. 3-53.

Hanna, Marwan
    1958   "The Lebanese in West Africa," *West Africa*, #2141 (April 26th).

Haddad, Safia
    1969   "The Woman's Role in Socialization of Syrian-Americans in Chicago," in Hagopian and Paden, *op. cit.*, pp. 84-101.

Hagopian, Elaine C.
    1969   "The Institutional Development of the Arab-American Community of Boston: A Sketch," in Hagopian and Paden, *op. cit.*, pp. 67-83.

Hitti, Philip
    1924   *Syrians In America*. New York: George Doran.

Houghton, Louise
    1911   "Syrians in the United States," *The Survey*. Vol. 26, Part I-July 1; Part II-August 5th; Part III-Sept. 2nd; Part IV-Oct. 7th.

    1969   "In Santiago Society, No One Cares If Your Name is Carey or De-Yrazaval," *New York Times*, Sept. 14th, p. 84.

Joseph, Suad
    1964   "Where the Twain Shall Meet: The Lebanese in Cortland County," *New York Folklore Quarterly*, 20:3, (Sept.), pp. 175-191.

Kasses, Assad S.
1972 "Cross Cultural Comparative Familism of a Christian Arab People," *Jl. of Marriage and the Family,* Vol. 34, #3 (August), pp. 539-544.

Katibah, Habib I
1946 *Arabic-speaking Americans.* New York: The Institute of Arab-American Affairs.

Kayal, Philip
1966 "Eastern Catholics See New Role in America," *Melkite Digest* 3:1 (Dec.-Jan.) pp. 5-7.

1967 "Eastern Christians in America: Problems in Dialogue," *Diakonia* 2:2, pp. 93-100.

1973 "Religion and Assimilation: Catholic 'Syrians' in America," *International Migration Review,* Vol. 7, No. 4 (Winter) pp. 409-426.

Karoub, Michael (ed.)
1962 Golden Jubilee Testimonial Program Honoring Hussein Karoub for Fifty Years to Islam and the American-Arab Communities in the U. S. and Canada. Detroit: Arab-American Printing Co.

Lacko, Michael
1964 "The Churches of Eastern Rite in North America," *Unitas* 16 (Summer), pp. 89-115.

Makdisi, Nadim
1962 "The Maronites in the Americas and in Atlanta," *Golden Jubilee Book, 1962.* Atlanta: Atlanta Maronite Community.

1966 "Arab Adventures in the New World," *Yearbook, 1965-66.* New York: The Action Committee on American Arab Relations.

Maloof, Louis
1962 *The Maronite Heritage Intact and Immaculate. In Defense of the Irish of the East.* Atlanta: Atlanta Maronite Community.

Miller, Lucius Hopkins
1904 *Our Syrian Population: A Study of the Syrian Population of Greater New York.* Columbia University Library, N. Y., and N. Y. Public Library, Widener Collection, Harvard University.

Mokarzel, Salloum
    1892   "A Picturesque Colony," *New York Tribune*, October 2nd; p. 21.

    1927   "History of the Syrains in New York," *New York American*, October 3rd.

    1947   "The People of New York," *Life*, February 17th; pp. 89-96.

Rice, Jack
    1967   "A Resurgence of a Lebanese Parish in St. Louis." *St. Louis Post Dispatch*, Nov. 27th, pp. 1-3.

Safa, Elie
    1916   "Syrians and Arabians In America," *American Review of Reviews*, November; pp. 533-534.

    1919   "Syrians in the United States," *Literary Digest*, May 3rd; p. 43.

    1960   *L'Emigration Libanaise*. (Beirut).

Sengstock, Mary C.
    1968   The Corporation and the Ghetto: An Analysis of the Effects of Corporate Retail Grocery Sales on Ghetto Life. *Journal of Urban Law*. 45:673-703.

    1970   Telkeif, Baghdad, Detroit-Chaldeans Blend Three Cultures. *Michigan History* 54:293-310.

Suleiman, Michael W.
    1969   "The New Arab-American Community," in Hagopian and Paden, *op. cit.*, pp. 37-49.

Tannous, Afif
    1941   "Social Change in an Arab Village," *American Sociological Review*. 6:5 (October), pp. 650-652.

    1942a   "Emigration as a Force of Social Change in an Arab Village," *Rural Sociology*, 7:1 (March), pp. 62-74.

    1942b   "Acculturation of an Arab-Syrian Community in the Deep South," *American Sociological Review*. 8:3 (June), pp. 264-271.

Treudley, Mary B.
    1953   "The Ethnic Group As A Collectivity," *Social Forces*, 31:3, (March), pp. 261-265.

1918   "Their First Impression of New York," *World Outlook*, (June).

Wakin, Edward
1974   *The Lebanese and Syrians in America*. Chicago: Claretian Publisher.

Wilson, Howard Barrett
1903   Notes on Syria Folk-Lore Collected in Boston. *Journal of American Folk-Lore* 16:133-147.

Winder, R. Bayly
1962   "The Lebanese Emigration in West Africa," *Comparative Studies In Society and History*, 4:3, pp. 296-333.

Wolf, C. Umhau
1960   Muslims in the American Mid-West, *The Muslim World*. Jan: 39-48.

Yazbek, Msgr. Joseph
1923   "The Syrians," *Catholic Builders of the Nation*. Boston: Continental Press, Inc.

Younis, Dr. Adele
1966   "The Arabs Who Followed Columbus," *Yearbook, 1965-66*. New York: Action Committee on American Arab Relations.

1969   "The Growth of Arabic-Speaking Settlements In the United States," in Hagopian and Paden, *op. cit.*, pp. 102-111.

UNPUBLISHED MATERIAL

Ahdab-Yehia, May
1970   'Some General Characteristics of the Lebanese Maronite Community in Detroit,' Wayne State University: Unpublished M.A. thesis.

Allhoff, John
1969   'Analysis of the Role of St. Raymond's Maronite Church as an Agent in the Assimilation of Lebanese Families in St. Louis.' University of Mississippi: Unpublished M.A. dissertation.

Al-Tahir, Abdul
1952   'The Arab Community in the Chicago Area: A Comparative Study of The Christian-Syrians and the Muslim Palestinians,' University of Chicago: Unpublished Ph.D. dissertation.

Al-Nouri, Qais Naim
1964   'Conflict and Persistence in the Iraqi-Chaldean Acculturation,'

University of Washington, Seattle: Unpublished Ph.D. dissertation.

David, J. K.
1954   'The Near East Settlers of Jacksonville and Duval County.' Paper presented at the annual meeting of the Jacksonville Historical Society, May 12, 1954, Jacksonville, Florida.

Dlin, Norman
1961   'Some Cultural and Geographic Aspects of the Christian Lebanese in Metropolitan Los Angeles,' University of California at Los Angeles: Unpublished M.A. thesis.

Elya, Rev. John
1965   "The Accommodation of a Socio-Religious Sub-System: The Melkite Catholics in the United States," Unpublished term report, Boston College.

Gasperetti. Eli
1948   'The Maronites: The Origin and Development of a Theocracy,' Columbia University: Unpublished M.A. thesis.

Kassees, Assad S.
1970   'The People of Ramallah: A People of Christian Arab Heritage.' Florida State University: Unpublished Ph.D. dissertation.

Kayal, Philip M.
1970   'The Churches of the Catholic Syrians and Their Role in the Assimilation Process.' Fordham University: Unpublished Ph.D. dissertation.

Knowlton, Clark S.
1955   'Spatial and Social Mobility of the Syrians and Lebanese in the City of Sao Paulo, Brazil,' Vanderbilt University: Unpublished Ph.D. dissertation.

Maloof, Louis J.
1958   'A Sociological Study of Arabic Speaking People in Mexico,' University of Florida: Unpublished Ph.D. dissertation.

Saba, Leila
1971   'The Social Assimilation of the Ramallah Community Residing in Detroit,' Wayne State University: Unpublished M.A. thesis.

Sengstock, Mary C.
1967   'Maintenance of Social Interaction Patterns in an Ethnic

Group,' Washington University: Unpublished Ph.D. dissertation.

Stein, Edith
1922   'Some Near Eastern Immigrant Groups in Chicago,' University of Chicago: Unpublished M.A. thesis.

Swanson, Jon C.
1970   'Mate Selection and Intermarriage in an American Arab Moslem Community,' University of Iowa: Unpublished M.A. thesis.

Tannous, Afif
1940   'Trends of Social and Cultural Change in Bishmizeen,' Cornell University: Unpublished Ph.D. dissertation.

Wakin, Edward
1974   The Lebanese and Syrians in America. Chicago: Claretian Publ.

Wasfi, A. A.
1970   'Dearborn Arab-Moslem Community: A Study of Acculturation.' Ann Arbor, Michigan: Michigan Microfilms.

Younis, Adele
1961   'The Coming of the Arabic-Speaking People to the United States,' Boston University: Unpublished Ph.D. dissertation.

Zelditch, Morris
1936   'The Syrians in Pittsburgh,' University of Pittsburgh: Unpublished M.A. thesis.

APPENDIX

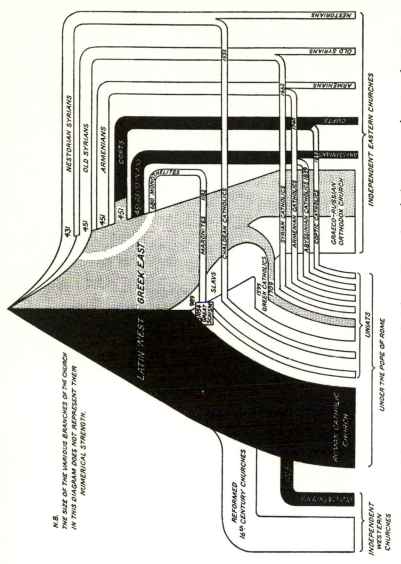

Main Schisms of the Christian Church with approximate dates.
(From G. Baer, Population & Society in the Arab East, Praeger, N.Y.,
1964, p. 85, as reproduced from C.T.Bridgeman, Religious Communities
in the Christian East, The Nile Mission Press, n.p., n.d.)